The Politzer Saga

By Linda Ambrus Broenniman

Bethesda Communications Group

Published by the **Bethesda Communications Group**
49 Wellesley Circle
Glen Echo, MD 20812
www.bcgpub.com

ISBN-13: 978-1-7367773-7-4
ISBN-10: 1-7367773-7-8

Cover and book design created by
Beatrix Kiss and Levente Tóth

Most of the photos in this book are from the
Ambrus / Politzer family collection. Photos from other
sources are credited in the photo inscriptions.

Dedicated To
ANDRÁS GYEKICZKI
1958 - 2020

Without András, this book would not have been possible. I am forever grateful for his intelligence, persistence, generosity of spirit in helping me find my lost family, and for being a friend I could trust on an uncertain journey. I miss him every day.

Contents

Introduction ———————————————————————— 9

Chapter 1 Family Secrets ———————————————— 13

Chapter 2 My Roadmap to the Past ————————— 21

Chapter 3 Eisik, Son of Moses ——————————— 27

Chapter 4 Móricz and Rachel —————————————— 37

Chapter 5 The Story of Ábrahám ———————————— 49

Chapter 6 Illés Politzer ———————————————— 71

Chapter 7 Ádám Politzer ——————————————————— 81

Chapter 8 Zsigmond Politzer —————————————— 103

Chapter 9 Illés Politzer's Children ——————— 121

Chapter 10 Jozefa Politzer Misner ——————————— 131

Chapter 11 Ignácz Misner ——————————————————— 143

Chapter 12 Gyula Politzer ——————————————————— 163

Chapter 13 Margit Misner Politzer ——————————— 175

Chapter 14 Sándor Ambrus ————————————————————— 205

Chapter 15 My Parents: Julian Ambrus and Clara Bayer ——— 221

Epilogue ——————————————————————————————— 243

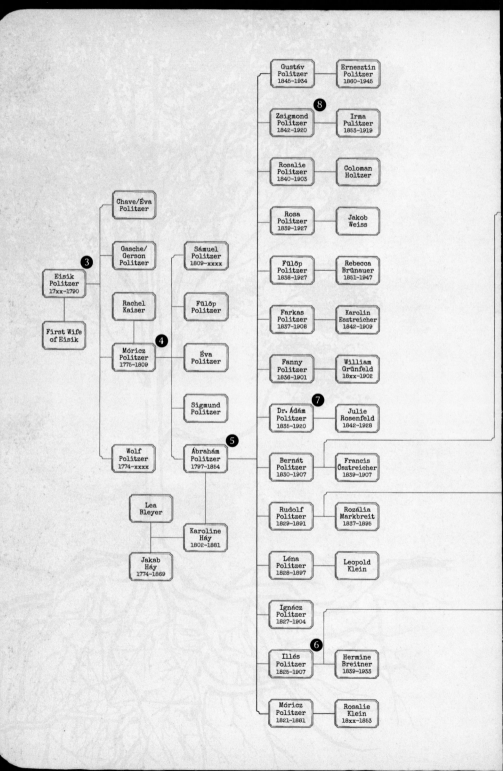

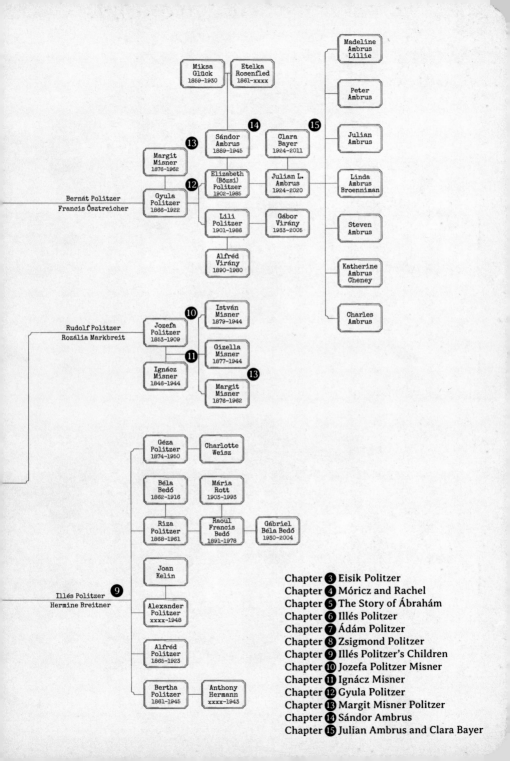

Miksa Glück 1859–1930
Etelka Rosenfled 1861–xxxx

Madeline Ambrus Lillie

Peter Ambrus

Julian Ambrus

Linda Ambrus Broenniman

Steven Ambrus

Katherine Ambrus Cheney

Charles Ambrus

13 Margit Misner 1876–1962

Bernát Politzer
Francis Ösztreicher

Gyula Politzer 1866–1922

14 Sándor Ambrus 1889–1945

15 Clara Bayer 1924–2011

12 Elizabeth (Bözsi) Politzer 1902–1985

Julian L. Ambrus 1924–2020

Lili Politzer 1901–1986

Gábor Virány 1933–2005

Alfréd Virány 1890–1980

Rudolf Politzer
Rozália Markbreit

10 Jozefa Politzer 1853–1909

István Misner 1879–1944

11 Gizella Misner 1877–1944

Ignácz Misner 1846–1944

13 Margit Misner 1876–1962

Géza Politzer 1874–1950

Charlotte Weisz

Béla Bedő 1862–1916

Mária Rott 1903–1993

Riza Politzer 1868–1961

Raoul Francis Bedő 1891–1978

Gábriel Béla Bedő 1930–2004

Joan Kelin

Illés Politzer
Hermine Breitner

9

Alexander Politzer xxxx–1948

Alfréd Politzer 1865–1923

Bertha Politzer 1861–1945

Anthony Hermann xxxx–1943

Chapter **3** Eisik Politzer
Chapter **4** Móricz and Rachel
Chapter **5** The Story of Ábrahám
Chapter **6** Illés Politzer
Chapter **7** Ádám Politzer
Chapter **8** Zsigmond Politzer
Chapter **9** Illés Politzer's Children
Chapter **10** Jozefa Politzer Misner
Chapter **11** Ignácz Misner
Chapter **12** Gyula Politzer
Chapter **13** Margit Misner Politzer
Chapter **14** Sándor Ambrus
Chapter **15** Julian Ambrus and Clara Bayer

Introduction

In 1949, my Hungarian parents crossed the ocean to start a new life. They had survived World War II, escaped a Stalinist regime, and finished their medical studies. They wanted to leave behind the pain and suffering. They wanted to start again. And they did, building successful careers as doctors in the United States. My six siblings and I were raised Catholic, in what was an idyllic American childhood.

When I was 27, I accidentally discovered that my father was Jewish. And that much of what I knew about him and his family was a lie. But I was young, not ready to embark on a journey to excavate the truth. Thirty-three years later, I could no longer ignore the yearning to know the truth that lay buried. It was time. Perhaps not too late, but almost. Many who knew the stories of my father's family could no longer remember them or had died.

I wonder now if a small measure of divine intervention allowed serendipity and good luck to cross my path during this difficult journey. Clues appeared when I needed them. In a box rescued from a fire in my parents' home, I found long hidden letters, photographs, and documents. Later I found memoirs written by family members.

I can't confirm divine intervention. But I know for sure that what I found was not possible without András Gyekiczki, a Hungarian lawyer, sociologist, and family researcher. With András, I was able to uncover my family history. Tracing my roots back to the 18th century, I learned how my ancestors came to have the last name Politzer and my father, Ambrus. I learned about other family names I had not previously known – Háy, Misner, Glück, Virány, Rosenfeld, Morgenstern, among them.

András shared our findings with friends and colleagues, including the director of the Hungarian Jewish Museum and Archives, and the deputy director of the Rumbach Street Synagogue Project. They encouraged him to write a proposal for the Rumbach Synagogue Exhibit.

András wrote, "I hardly know any non-fiction sagas to better exemplify Hungarian Jewish fate of the past 300 years as this Politzer-Misner-Ambrus-Virány story. All that fantastic talent, diligence, and readiness to act for and during the birth of modern Hungary. All those sufferings, torture and misery they went through..."

The Rumbach Synagogue, built in 1872, had been one of Budapest's most prominent synagogues. Damaged during the Holocaust, it continued to decay for decades, until the Federation of Hungarian Jewish Communities (MAZSIHISZ) and the Budapest Jewish Community (BZSH) raised state and private funding for its renovation.

As part of the renovation plan, the vision was to have an education and cultural center on the Synagogue's third floor. Themes would include issues relevant to the lives of many Jewish families in Hungary today: unmasking family origins, secrecy and denial of family history, Jewish identity, and coexistence.

And so the exhibit came to be. The Rumbach Synagogue re-opened on June 10, 2021. The Politzer Saga Exhibit opened two months later. I discovered that my great-great-uncle Zsigmond Politzer owned seats there. The struggles, tragedies, and triumphs of my father's Jewish family, lost for so long, are now visible in the light of day. Hidden no more.

The elegance and beauty with which my family stories are visualized and told in the Exhibit is deeply gratifying. I began my journey to find lost family. To find them, after so long, brought them back to life for me. To realize that their stories are a way to bring Hungarian history to life, is a tribute to them that I had never anticipated.

For me, telling their stories, writing this book, made them feel real, like people I wished I had known. As I learned about their everyday lives, and pieced together events that were meaningful to them, it helped me feel I was part of them. We are separated by space and time, but hearts joined, we are family.

"

To learn means to accept the postulate that life did not begin at my birth. Others have been here before me, and I walk in their footsteps. The books I have read were composed by generations of fathers and sons, mothers and daughters, teachers and disciples. I am the sum total of their experiences, their quests.

"

ELIE WIESEL

Chapter 1

Family Secrets

Longing for the Truth

I am the middle child of seven American children born to Hungarian physicians, Clara and Julian Ambrus, who survived World War II and began a new life in the US during the 1950s. We were raised Catholic in Buffalo, New York and attended church regularly with our parents. It was a happy childhood. A charmed life. But there were secrets.

In my late twenties, (in the early 1980s), the godmother to my oldest sister revealed, through a slip of the tongue, that my father was Jewish. I began to wonder what else I might not know. Not long after that revelation, in 1984 and 1990, I learned more about my parents' past when I traveled to Budapest with them. Yet larger truths remained hidden.

One such truth emerged in 2006: We received news that the Israeli Government was honoring my Catholic mother as Righteous Among the Nations, an honor recognizing non-Jews "who acted according to the noblest principles of humanity by risking their lives to save Jews during the Holocaust." Her name is inscribed on the wall at Yad Vashem (the World Holocaust Remembrance Center in Israel) along with more famous names, such as Oskar Schindler, Raoul Wallenberg, and Irena Sandler. My mother risked her life to save Jews, my father and my grandmother among them. I was so proud, but also stunned to realize how little I knew of my parents' true history. And that I knew nothing about my father's Jewish family. My Jewish family. Or about my own grandmother – my father's mother who escaped Hungary during the 1956 revolution and came to Buffalo to live with and help care for us, her grandchildren. She was big-hearted and spoiled us. Like my father, she was an expert storyteller, but she never revealed anything about the true history of her life.

After the ceremony that honored my mother, I broke the unwritten rule that governed discourse at our house: no questions about the past. My father continued to deflect until his death, and my mother was in the later stages of Alzheimer's. On one occasion, though, my mother's answer surprised me. She responded that a box with documents held answers. My quest for the truth about my family began at that moment.

Truth in the Ashes

I was amazed she remembered this detail when she remembered so little. But when I could not find such a box anywhere, I began to wonder if the box had existed only in her imagination.

In February 2011 my parents' home caught fire. My father survived with minor burns. My mother, after 12 excruciating days in coma, succumbed. I presumed the box she remembered had burned, if it ever existed.

Five years after the fire, my sister Madeline called to say she had found a box among the items rescued from the fire. She was sending it out the next day.

It arrived looking like any U-Haul moving box. I opened it nervously. Its musty odor reminded me of an attic closed off to fresh air for decades. It was filled with dog-eared files stuffed with papers and manila envelopes of photos. The documents were mostly in Hungarian or German. Most were dated from the 1930s and 1940s; some photos, postcards, and documents bore dates from the late 1800s and early 1900s. Amazingly, they had survived World War I, World War II, the Hungarian Revolution of 1956, and the fire in my parents' home.

Buried deep within the box I found a black marbled composition book, bearing the words "Our Family Tree" on the cover. No author was identified. Much to my relief, it was written in English. Ábrahám Politzer (1797-1854) began the list of names. The irony of his name did not escape me - Abraham was the first patriarch in the Old Testament, progenitor of the Jewish nation. I had found our own Ábrahám, a Jewish patriarch in my family. Names, dates, and relationships were listed. Occasionally a brief description was included. It identified Politzer descendants through six generations, including me and my six siblings. I wondered who had written it as I read and leafed through the handwritten book.

I learned that in the mid 1800s Ábrahám and his wife Karoline raised a large family of fourteen children. Many more relatives followed. By the time I finished putting them into my newly purchased ancestry software (Legacy and ancestry.com), I had discovered over 300 names. The descriptions, though meager, made them come to life for me, but also left me yearning to learn more.

I was almost certain that Gábor Virány, my father's cousin had compiled the book. Gábor had a remarkable memory and was fluent in English. Growing up in Hungary, my father and Gábor, both only children, were like brothers. They lived in separate apartments in the same building on Teréz körút (körút means boulevard) in Budapest.

Gábor was autistic. He remembered everything: names, relationships, birthdates, marriage dates. He remembered dates of any significance and those that were not. My parents and I visited him in Budapest in 1984 and 1990. Asked about an event like a concert from decades ago, he recounted the weather, food served, music played, and what guests wore. As I later learned, when Gábor died in 2005, his niece sent his belongings to my father. The box my sister sent included some of the items Gábor had kept throughout his life. Without it, I could not have pieced together our family history.

History: Lost and Found

The contents of the box would bring me closer to the truth about my family, but the path to discovery is rarely a straight line. There are twists and turns, and disappointing dead ends. It requires a relentless commitment to finding answers and overcoming obstacles, especially when the lights at the end of the tunnel are answers to questions that no one wants to ask.

Using Microsoft translator, I was able to identify birth certificates, marriage certificates, and death certificates. But even simple translations were far from perfect and often created more questions than answers. Searching for help, I was introduced to Anna Bayer, a Hungarian Jewish expat who lived a half hour's drive from my home in Virginia. Anna was passionate about Hungary and Hungarian Jewish history. When she opened the door, I was instantly drawn to her enthusiasm and warmth. She took me to her basement where three large cloth panels were displayed. These had been used in an exhibit organized by András Gyekiczki to showcase the vibrant pre-war Jewish community in the town of Pápa, Hungary. Of the 3,600 residents, only 200 survived the war.

The next six hours were enlightening and deeply emotional. Anna's descriptions provided a rich subtext to the documents. Some of them, including letters written to government officials, were historically significant and important to research. I would need much more than a translator. I needed to find someone who understood historical context and meaning.

She said she would introduce me to András, her trusted friend. András had degrees in law and sociology. In the post-communist era and the early formation of a democratic government after the fall of the Iron Curtain in 1990, he had held various government positions, including chief of staff to the Minister of Interior of Hungary and chief of staff for the Mayor of Budapest. He was a disciplined researcher with the skills to help me find my family.

Connecting the Dots

Anna was right. András was an amazing sleuth, a master of connecting the dots to lead us to more discoveries. From the names and dates on gravestones, he explored birth, death, and marriage records, most handwritten in ancient registers.

Ironically, cemeteries became the place where my family felt most alive to me. Their names were etched into the gravestones with dates, names of spouses or other family members, an epitaph, or some remembrance written by a loved one. Proof that they had lived and died. That they had really been of this place.

Each clue led to the next. András uncovered century-old donation books and tablets, tax ledgers, land certificates, election registers, school reports. He found newspaper advertisements, articles written by or about a relative, a name mentioned in a book, or a book written by a relative. He found documents in unexpected places.

Just locating names was no small task. In the Austro-Hungarian Empire, educated Jews typically spoke three languages: Yiddish amongst themselves, Hungarian when chatting with their neighbors, and Austrian (German) in front of the authorities. A fourth, Latin, was also spoken. To my surprise, until 1844, Latin had been Hungary's official language.

When recording a Jewish birth, marriage, or death, any of these languages might have been used, resulting in different names for the same person. For example, a certificate found in the box was dated November 7th, 1941, signed by Rabbi Dr. József Borsodi of Kecskemét. He confirmed that in various registers the family name "Politzer" was recorded in several different ways: Pulicer, Puliczer, Pullitzer, Pollitzer and Pulliczer. András checked and rechecked such details to ensure the accuracy of his findings.

Treasures from the Past

András also pursued the living, tracking down the descendants of relatives and friends mentioned in books and letters. He visited with Gábor's niece, Kati Erényi, at her home in Budapest. Her gift of two books greatly enriched our findings.

The first book, typeset and written in German, was titled *Die Geschichte unserer Familie* (*Our Family History*). Written by Zsigmond Politzer (1842-1920), the second youngest of Ábrahám's fourteen children, it tells the story of the Politzer family beginning in the early 1700s with Ábrahám's grandfather, Eisik, and ending with Zsigmond's own story. From the book, I learned about seven generations of my Politzer ancestors, including those Zsigmond would have known who were born in the Austro-Hungarian Empire before World War I.

The second book, titled *Az újabbik Balogh* (*The new tailor Balogh*), was written by Gábor and translated by András. It chronicles Gábor's experiences from the middle of 1943 until the summer of 1945, after the end of World War II. It is a window into the world through the lens of a nine-year-old autistic boy. Embedded in his detailed descriptions of clothes and food, Gábor reveals the lives of the Politzer, Misner, Ambrus and Virány families during World War II and the toll the war took on them.

Survival: A Family Saga

These books coupled with András' research provided a rich history of Jewish survival in Hungary in the 18th, 19th and 20th centuries.

Politzer, Misner, Glück, Háy, Morgenstern, Rosenfeld. These are family names I came to learn about. They are not well-known names like Rothchild, Arnstein, Pulitzer, Soros. Yet, my ancestors crossed paths with those famous families. Their status and achievements, however, did not insulate them from historical events. Over and over again, they were battered by religious persecution, wars, epidemics, and economic upheavals that almost destroyed them. I learned of their struggles, their bravery, and their accomplishments. Of their generosity of spirit and remarkable resilience.

András once wrote to me, "I hardly know any non-fiction sagas to better exemplify Hungarian Jewish fate of the past 300 years as this Politzer, Misner, Ambrus, Virány story ... All those sufferings, torture and misery they went through."

A Gift of Truth

It wasn't enough to find the family my father never spoke of. I needed to write their stories. It was a way to connect to their lives and to make them even more real. By writing about them, I began to understand where my siblings and I came from.

With this book I honor our ancestors' memory. And I experience the true meaning of the Jewish statement of condolence (often expressed after the death of a loved one), "May their memory be for a blessing."

Chapter 2

My Roadmap to the Past

Zsigmond Politzer writes Our Family History

In the 1870s, Zsigmond (the 13th of Ábrahám Politzer's 14 children) traveled often between Vienna and Budapest. He had family, homes, and businesses in both cities. On one particular train trip, he sat next to a rather talkative gentleman, who he learned was a distant relative. The gentleman mentioned that his father and grandfather often talked about the life of the Politzers. He wondered why no one of the "very talented and intelligent people amongst you" had written the history of this "remarkable family, as it would be a beautiful and very interesting book."

Inspired by the conversation, Zsigmond quickly discovered how difficult it was to research family history and to write a book. "In a normal family like ours, where there is no written information, you have to rely on the word-of-mouth details regarding family traditions and heritage. These, however, need to be considered carefully, as I only want to write about true events, not some novel."

In Kittsee, Austria (Köpcsény in Hungarian), Zsigmond found an old rabbi who had gone to school with his father's younger brother. The rabbi had lived next door to the Politzer family and run errands for Zsigmond's grandmother, Rachel. He remembered the family stories that she told him. The rabbi suggested that Zsigmond go to see a retired priest. The priest took Zsigmond to the Jewish cemetery where he knew every grave. He pointed out three headstones. The first two were of Zsigmond's great-grandfather, Eisik, and his wife. Although they were half sunken in the ground, the date of Eisik's passing, 1790, could still be read. The third headstone, still intact, was Zsigmond's grandfather, Móricz. Later, Zsigmond commissioned another red marble headstone with real gold letters that read "Móricz Politzer, Doctor in Kittsee, died 1809" to replace the old sandstone one.

Jewish Cemetery in Kittsee, Austria

Zsigmond's quest had its stops and starts. "Due to hundreds of obligations, such as raising my own family, business and so forth, the project of writing a book fell in the background for a long time." In 1900, however, more than two decades after Zsigmond had begun work on his book, business took him to Moravia where he learned more about the family in Nikolsburg (currently Mikulov, Czech Republic). Subsequently, through correspondence with rabbis from Politz (Czech Republic), Zalaegerszeg (Hungary), Abony and Irsa (Hungary), he gathered the information captured in *Our Family History*.

Truth and Family Devotion

Zsigmond wrote, "From 1912 onwards I experienced some physical ailments, and I restarted the work as I was afraid 'to die before I get but half so high.' I hastily jotted down everything I knew and left it in Kornél's hands, my son, who has a sense of family and a warm heart, in the hope that he would be able to make sense out of my notes to create a book of our family history, Wahrheit und Dichtung (Truth and Poetry) for our children and grandchildren."

This short book (47 pages) is the basis for several stories I tell. They are enriched by the historical context András helped me add. Echoing Zsigmond's wishes, I wanted to write only the truth about true events. To bring their stories back into the light.

In 2022, I searched for Móricz's tombstone, but time had eroded the inscriptions and made them unreadable.

Die Geschichte

unserer

Familie

Motto:

Wie Schwer sind nicht die Mittel zu erwerben
Durch die man zu den Quellen steigt
Und eh man mir den halben Weg erreicht,
Muss wohl ein armer Teufel sterben.

/ Goethe: Faust./

Vorwort.

Als ich in den siebziger Jahren des XIX. Jahrhunderts von Wien
nach Budapest reiste, fuhr ich in einem Halbcuppée, allein mit
einem Bekannten, der Vorgab, ein enfernter Verwandter zu sein.
Der Herr war sehr gesprächig und liess die Bemerkung fallen,
sein Vater und Grossvater erzählten oft Episoden aus dem Leben
der Politzer, dass er sich wundere, dass unter den vielen begab-
ten und intellegenten Menschen, "unter Euch" sich noch keiner
gefunden habe, der die Geschichte dieser merkwürdigen Familie
schriebe. Es gäbe dies ein sehr schönes und interessantes Buch.-
Ich verabschiedete mich in Budapest, und, wie man Reisegespräche
vergisst, dachte ich über diese Unterhaltung nicht weiter nach.-
Einige Tage nachher aber setzte sich diese Idee in meinem Kopfe
fest, sie gefiel mir, und bald reifte in mir der Entschluss, den
Versuch zu wagen. Ich wusste nicht, wie ich die Sache abfassen
solle. Vorerst hiess es Notizen machen über Vorfälle, von denen
Menschen, die in der Familie lebten, Kenntnis haben mochten. We-
nige, ziemlich unbedeutende Begebenheiten wusste ich von meinem
Bruder Moritz, der schon damals sehr leidend war, mehr durch Bruder
Bernát; so viel war mir aber klar, dass ich in Kittsee, dem Wohn-
orte des Grossvaters, vieles erfahren werde, zu mindesten die Rich-
tung finden werde, in der ich mich zu bewegen habe. Die Schwie-
rigkeiten waren gross. Bei alten, adeligen Geschlechtern, die

Cover and First Page of
Our Family History written
by Zsigmond Politzer.

Chapter 3

Eisik, Son of Moses

Eisik (birthdate unknown, in the 1700s – 1790), Zsigmond's great grandfather, was also my great-great-great-great-great-great-grandfather (eight generations before me) on my father's side of the family.

It was during the reign of the Austro-Hungarian Emperor Charles VI, at the beginning of the 18th century, that Eisik was born to Moses. Moses lived in Northern Bohemia (present day Czech Republic) where he traded linen from Saxony, a center of the linen industry.

As the linen trade grew in international importance, Moses prospered. He became wealthy enough to pay for music lessons for Eisik. Bohemia was well known for its music. The village schools, run by Jesuits, included music as a core part of the curriculum. Students were taught violin, oboe, and bassoon. Moses noticed Eisik's talent for music at an early age and hired a well-known musician to give him violin lessons. Eisik made such progress that whenever he played at home, people would gather outside to listen.

Itinerant Life

In 1727, Emperor Charles VI issued the Familiants Laws, which limited the number of Jewish families who could legally reside in a particular locality. It stipulated that only one son from any household could obtain the right to marry and establish a family. These laws, meant to curtail the growing Jewish population, stayed in effect well over one hundred years, until the Revolutions of 1848 (which spread throughout Europe), stifling economic growth and social mobility in Jewish communities.

Moses was unable to settle in one place for any length of time. Discrimination and taxation forced Jews to move constantly in search of a better life. As Moses amassed more wealth, the rural judges demanded more money. Eventually Moses moved his family to Politz. (See **map**. Most likely the name was Pullitz). We don't know when Moses passed away after they settled there, but when he did Eisik took over his father's business.

The Wandering Violinist

Our story begins one Friday afternoon in the year 1740, the first year of Empress Maria Theresa's reign (1740-1780). A devout Catholic, Maria Theresa called the Jews a "plague on this race" and instituted even more repressive policies and oppressive taxation on the Jews than her father, Charles VI.

Although Eisik became a linen merchant like his father, his first love remained the violin. He gave private concerts for his friends and neighbors. The whole town spoke of how beautifully this young man played. His landlord, a miller who lived in the house across the street, was one of Eisik's biggest fans.

The miller had been told about a new musical piece, described as being "so heavenly" it sounded as if the angels in heaven were playing. He asked Eisik to play this piece at the beginning of Shabbat, the Jewish day of rest. Because it was forbidden to play a musical instrument on Shabbat, Eisik refused. The miller offered Eisik a sack of flour. Eisik refused his offer. When gifts failed, he threatened to evict Eisik from his house. Eisik stood his ground. The argument escalated. The miller insulted his Jewish faith. Finally, Eisik threw him out. But before slamming the door, Eisik shouted, "Even if your Lord Jesus came, I would not play tonight."

Incensed, the miller went to the pastor of the local church and told him that the Jew, Eisik, had used the Lord's name in vain. The pastor reported the case to the church elders in Prague. They ordered an investigation.

18th century synagogue in Politz (Police u Jemnice, Czech Republic). Eisik most likely worshipped here. Photo courtesy of Ruth Ellen Gruber.

As the weeks went by, the miller regretted his actions and mended his relationship with Eisik. It seemed as though the incident would pass without repercussions until the pastor informed the miller that an execution team was on its way from Prague to arrest Eisik and take him to the church prison. They had not decided on his sentence: to cut out his tongue or burn him at the stake. The pastor requested that the miller keep this quiet. Eisik seemed to have many admirers, especially women admirers, among the villagers. The pastor worried that one of Eisik's admirers would try to save him before "justice" was served.

Shocked, the miller decided that he would save Eisik from such a fate. Thank goodness, or I would not be telling this story. After sundown, the miller went over to Eisik's house to warn him about the execution team. He gave Eisik money and urged him to leave that night.

So began Eisik's many years of wandering. With only a small sack and his violin, he left Politz forever. His violin enabled him to earn food and lodging as he wandered aimlessly for days. He finally reached Nikolsburg (see **map**) on the Moravian-Austrian border where his mother's distant relatives lived. In the 18th century, Nikolsburg became the largest Jewish settlement in Moravia and the Jewish population of 3,000 comprised half the town's inhabitants. Only a small number of Jews were allowed to make their living as artisans. The rest had to become merchants. The Jewish community experienced even greater hardships than restrictions on their choice of livelihood. Empress Maria Theresa imposed heavy taxes on the community to pay for the Silesian wars.

Nikolsburg Jewish Quarter – 19th Century. Courtesy of the National Heritage Institute, regional office Brno, Czech Republic.

Painting of Nikolsburg Chevra Kadisha (Jewish Burial Society) circa 1780. From the collection of the Jewish Museum in Prague.

Austro-Hungarian Empire
13th century

Main

Ohře

Cheb

Elbe

① Prague

BOHEMIA

Neckar

German Empire

Vltava

MORA

Brno

②

③

④

Danube

Danube

Isar

Inn

Lech

Vienna

Salzburg

AUSTRIA

⑦ Sopron

Innsbruck

Mur

TYROL

Graz

Raab

Klagenfurt

Maribor

Adda

Trento

CARNIOLA

Sava

Ljubljana

Zagreb

Trieste

CROATIA-

Adige

Rijeka

Una

Sar

Po

Italy

Banja

BO

Zadar

DALMATIA

HER

① Northern Bohemia = Western Czech Republic
② Politz = Police u Jemnice, Czech Republic
③ Nikolsburg = Mikulov, Czech Republic
④ Pressburg = Bratislava, Slovakia
⑤ Sátoraljaújhely, Zemplén County, Hungary
⑥ Napkor, Szabolcs County, Hungary
⑦ Kittsee/Köpcsény, Hungary = Kittsee, Austria

Fortunately, one of Eisik's relatives gave him asylum in his home and employed him in his business, most likely a merchant business. Eisik was a good and loyal employee. Soon he was trusted enough to take business trips as far away as Hungary.

At home in Nikolsburg, everyone delighted in listening to Eisik's beautiful music. Once again, however, his playing got him into trouble. This time it was about the love of a woman. A Croatian tanner's daughter fell head over heels in love with Eisik. And he with her. He convinced her to convert to Judaism. He convinced a young rabbi to marry them. His bride's father, the tanner, pressed charges against Eisik as soon as he learned about the marriage, And so Eisik, this time with his wife, was on the run again. Evading Eisik's father-in-law, they were on the constant move.

Their next destination was Pressburg (known as Pozsony in Hungarian, today Bratislava, Slovakia, see **map**). Pressburg, situated on the Danube, was a large and important town – the coronation site and legislative center of the Kingdom of Hungary. I could imagine that Eisik's reputation as a brilliant violin virtuoso spread throughout the town and beyond. Despite 60 miles of poor roads that made travel difficult between Nikolsburg and Pressburg, it did not take long for Eisik's father-in-law to catch up with them.

The couple next fled to Zemplen County, almost 300 miles from Pressburg (see **map**), a harrowing journey across the Tatra Mountains (the highest mountain range in the Carpathian Mountains). The distance and rugged terrain likely deterred his father-in-law from further pursuit. Little is known about their lives in Zemplen County.

Perhaps Eisik became a merchant, trading in the famous Tokay wines of the area. The only thing we know: the couple gave birth to their first son, Wolf, in the capital city of Sátoraljaújhely. Two more sons followed, Móricz and Gasche/Gerson.

Their daughter Chave (Eva) was born in Szabolcs County on the northern edge of the Great Hungarian Plain (see **map**). Eisik's wife died giving birth to Chave and was buried in Szabolcs. Zsigmond wrote: "The woman who had risked and sacrificed everything lastly had to pay for her life for loving Eisik." Her father's death pre-dated hers. The father left his inheritance to the church.

Kittsee

Some years after his wife's death, Eisik wanted to return west, to the area where he had met his wife. He returned alone. I presume he went in advance to make sure his decision was a good one, before subjecting his children to the long and difficult journey. Eventually, his four children joined him.

They settled in Kittsee, six miles south of Pressburg. Kittsee belonged to the "Seven Holy Communities," under the protection of Prince Paul Esterházy. In the 17th and 18th centuries, landholding aristocrats granted Jews rights to residence, the pursuit of certain occupations, and the maintenance of religious institutions in return for certain obligations and payments (protection money). The Esterházy family was one of the wealthiest and most influential in the Austrian empire. They were well-known for their patronage of musicians, and in their castle at Eisenstadt, they had a well-appointed orchestra where Joseph Haydn served as music director from 1766-1790.

Esterházy Palace, a focal point for music where Joseph Hayden served as musical director from 1766-1790. Eisenstadt, Austria.

Kittsee, Vienna, and Eisenstadt formed a triangle, each about 40 miles from the other. With musicians such as Mozart, Salieri, and Beethoven living in Vienna, I imagine it would have been a triangle well traversed by musicians seeking to participate in the performances of the day. I wonder if Eisik might have been one of these musicians. I like to think he was.

The wealthy Jewish community living in Vienna invited Eisik to be cantor on holidays. It was an honor.

The 40-plus years of wandering had ended. In Kittsee, Eisik married again, this time to a young widow, the daughter of a merchant whose last name was Figdor. András discovered that Eisik's new wife was an ancestor of József Joachim (1831-1907), one of Hungary's most famous violinists. As a result, music became an even more powerful force in Eisik's family.

Eisik's oldest son, Wolf, left his father's house at an early age to become an apprentice to a merchant in Pressburg. Later, Móricz, the second oldest, studied to become a surgeon. The younger son became a soldier. Of the daughter, nothing was mentioned in Zsigmond Politzer's account.

Eisik Becomes Eisik Politzer

All his life, Eisik had been known as Eisik son of Moses. Most Jews, except for the wealthy, did not have surnames, using a patronym to identify themselves.

In 1782, Emperor Joseph II, Maria Theresa's eldest son and successor, passed the "Edict of Tolerance" (see: **The 1782 Edict of Tolerance on page 35**). As part of this edict, for purposes of tax control, all Jews in the Habsburg Empire were ordered to acquire family names in the German language. They were given until 1787 to comply.

In practice, Jews could rarely choose their own surnames; the authorities did it for them. In Kittsee, judges decided the names on the basis of the given Jew's financial status. Wealthy Jews were given "good" names, such as Goldstein (golden stone) and Silverstein (silver stone). Some names referred to one's occupation (Fleishman: butcher, Schmidt: smith) or physical or personal traits (Grossman: large, Redlich: honest). Zsigmond described those less fortunate got names such as Kieselstein (gravestone). The most common practice was to use the town or region where they were born or where they currently lived. In compliance with the law, the name Politzer was bestowed upon Eisik.

"Judging by the last name Politzer (from Politz) Eisik must have been a poor man." So wrote Zsigmond Politzer in *Our Family History*.

We don't know how Eisik died or his age when he died, only that he died in 1790. He did not live long enough to see his children marry or meet his grandchildren.

LEARNING MORE

The 1782 Edict of Tolerance

Emperor Joseph II, Maria Theresa's eldest son and successor, was an admirer of Voltaire and a disciple of the school of enlightenment. With the intention of modernizing the empire, he set out to assimilate Jews into the broader social strata for both social and economic reasons. In 1782, he passed the Edict of Tolerance, which permitted Jewish children to attend schools and universities, eliminated vocational restrictions for Jewish adults, abolished stigmatizing rules of dress (gold badges, the precursor to yellow stars). Not all edicts were favorable, especially to the lower classes. The use of Yiddish and Hebrew was confined to the private sphere and restrictions on Jews owning property were maintained. Nevertheless, these edicts were the most advanced in Europe.

For the most part, the wealthy and educated Jews enthusiastically accepted the edicts. The poorer and lower classes were less than enthusiastic, as the edicts impinged upon language and specific Jewish laws and customs, such as marriage, divorce, burial, and the authority of the rabbinic courts. It prohibited large gatherings, making it difficult to establish a synagogue or form a community organization. Furthermore, Jews could now be conscripted into military service, a burden that fell heavily upon the lower classes.

To enable tax control and registration, Emperor Joseph II ordered all Jews to acquire family names in the German language.

FAMILY TREE

Chapter 4

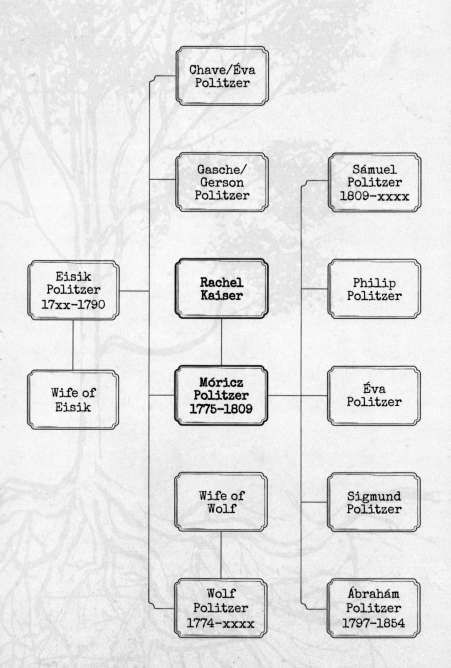

Móricz and Rachel

Móricz (1775-1809) was Eisik's second son, Zsigmond's grandfather, and my great-great-great-great-great-grandfather (seven generations before me). His wife, Rachel, a woman before her time, was highly educated. Móricz was the first physician in the family. Two of his grandsons followed in his footsteps, as well as many more in the generations to come, including my father and three of my siblings.

Medicine: A Family Legacy Begins

Zsigmond wrote in *Our Family History* that while Eisik was living in Kittsee, Móricz decided to become a surgeon. He enrolled at the University of Vienna in the faculty of medicine, though the year is not known.

Some years earlier, in 1745, Empress Maria Theresa had summoned the Dutch physician Gerard van Swieten (1700-1772) to transform the Austrian health service and medical university education. Under his guidance the Vienna Medical School attained international attention and became a major European medical research center. With Emperor Joseph II's Edict of Toleration (1782), Jews were allowed to study medicine and law. According to Zsigmond, Móricz was trained by the best experts of his time.

After his training, Móricz set up practice in Kittsee. A talented doctor, he also had a deep understanding of human character.

Josephinum, built 1783-1785. The first medical-surgical academy in Vienna, where Móricz received his medical degree. Courtesy of Josephinum – Ethics, Collections and History of Medicine, MedUni, Vienna.

Tall, strong, and handsome, "With his black stockings, tailcoat, and rice-powdered rococo pigtail, he was an impressive presence, as my father (Ábrahám) told us," Zsigmond wrote. "He was well liked by all because of his integrity and affable demeanor." Further, according to Zsigmond, "the young doctor was said to achieve miraculous recoveries" for Jews and Christians alike who came from afar to see him.

A Growing Reputation

Count Pálffy had such trust in Doctor Móricz Politzer, that he often sent his carriage to bring him back to Vienna, 40 miles west of Kittsee. The Pálffy ab Erdőd family were wealthy nobles of Hungarian descent with a long history of protecting Jews. In 1670, many of the Jews expelled from Vienna settled in the Pressburg suburbs of Schlossberg and Zuckermandel, towns that belonged to the Pálffys. Having Count Pálffy recommend Móricz to his wealthy associates as a skilled healer must have been an important asset. One of those introductions was to the banker Nathan Ádám von Arnstein from the banking house Arnstein and Eskeles in Vienna.

As the coronation site and legislative center of the Kingdom of Hungary, Pressburg was a thriving, important city in the early 1700s. Many court Jews, such as Simon Michael Pressburger, settled in the city. Court Jews were wealthy financiers to the nobles. In return for lending money, often for provisions and munitions to support the wars of the times, they were allowed to live in the cities. By advising monarchs, they often had significant influence on economic policy.

The family of Count Nikolaus Pálffy von Erdöd. The Count was a champion for Dr. Móricz Politzer. Painted by Martin van Meytens the Younger circa 1760. Photo: Johannes Stoll / Belvedere Museum, Vienna.

With the Edict of Tolerance, some restrictions on Jewish residency were lifted and by the end of the century more than 2,000 Jews lived in Pressburg. The city became an important center of Jewish learning – home to the Chassam Sofer Yeshiva (academy for Talmudic study), later to emerge as the most influential in central Europe, attracting eminent rabbis from far and wide.

An Extraordinary Woman

Móricz often travelled to Pressburg, about six miles from Kittsee. Esteemed and wealthy, he socialized with the elite of the Jewish community, often at the house of Moses Leitersdorfer, a banker and merchant. There, Móricz met his future wife, Rachel (Ráhel/Rechele) Kaiser, who was Moses Leitersdorfer's distant relative and adopted daughter.

Rachel was petite and very beautiful, but also frail. The Leitersdorfers raised her as a princess, in great luxury, as if she had been their child. As told by Zsigmond, how they came to adopt her was an extraordinary story, which I will briefly recount here.

Rachel was the youngest of four children. She was the only daughter of a bookstore proprietor, Joseph Kaiser, who lived in Zalaegerszeg, a city in western Hungary.

Rachel's eldest brother, an adventurer, traveled penniless to America and returned with a huge fortune. Ambitious and emboldened by success, her brother convinced his family to convert from Judaism to Christianity and emigrate to America. The plan had to be kept secret. The town had a strong, wealthy, and culturally rich Jewish community that would have prevented their conversion by legal, or even illegal, means. Rachel's father, Joseph, persuaded a Catholic priest to baptize the family.

Rachel refused. She did not want to be baptized nor did she want to go to America. In the middle of the night, she fled from her father's home to the home of a nearby family. The rest of her family left Zalaegerszeg without her and without being discovered.

This escapade became public in Jewish circles throughout the country. The Jewish community had great empathy for Rachel, impressed that such a young girl had the courage and conviction to resist her father and to oppose Catholic conversion.

Artistic rendering of the Trial
of Rachel. Unknown artist.
Courtesy of András Gyekiczki.

The Austro-Hungarian government, particularly during Emperor Joseph II's reign, encouraged Jews to convert to Catholicism, granting them certain privileges (citizenship at no cost) in exchange. For wealthy Jews, ennoblement was often the reward. By Imperial Law, children of baptized fathers were automatically baptized, even without their mother's permission. Rachel was a minor (most likely under 14). Rachel's father had become a Christian, and so the law required her to convert.

The Jewish community, including Rachel's relatives, contested this mandate. As Zsigmond wrote, "This created a big commotion throughout the whole land." The case rose up in the courts from the local authorities to the central legislative body. Finally, it came to the attention of Emperor Francis II. Francis II, considered to be a man of narrow views and limited vision, repealed many of Joseph II's reforms and introduced new restrictions, especially on the Jews of Vienna. That Francis would have been involved with such a case when he was struggling with Napoleon, the French Revolutionary Wars, and various Jacobin conspiracies, is extraordinary.

Emperor Francis II decided that Rachel must choose between the two religions for herself. A special commission was appointed. It was ordered that on a certain day, time, and place in Zalaegerszeg, Jews would line up on the left, Christians would line up on the right, and Rachel would have to walk between them. At the end, whichever side she stood on would indicate the choice she would abide by for the rest of her life. At the end, she stood on the left, choosing Judaism. The rabbi attending the process blessed her, saying that all her descendants would be good and happy people.

My eyes welled up when I read this story. I was one of Rachel's descendants, her great-great-great-great-great-granddaughter. I sighed, grateful that her courage and convictions were rewarded with such a blessing.

Moses Leitersdorfer, hearing about this event, made the long and difficult journey to Zalaegerszeg (about 100 miles) to meet Rachel. He took her home to Pressburg, adopted her, and gave her the best education possible. Moses quickly learned to appreciate Rachel's honest and strong character and her intellectual gifts. She was an exceptional student. The Latin language was her favorite. As Zsigmond wrote, "It is safe to say that in all of Hungary there was not another such educated Jewish woman." Even at a very old age, when she lived in Irsa (in Hungary), people would come from all over to converse with her in Latin, including a Catholic priest and the Emperor's bodyguard, Peter Szabó.

Love at First Sight

Móricz, a highly regarded doctor, probably had many women admirers. But it was at the Leitersdorfer home, a gathering place for Pressburg Jewish society, that he met and fell in love with Rachel. Rachel reciprocated his love. Moses approved of the union, and they married in 1795. By that time, Móricz's father Eisik had passed away.

The marriage was a happy one. They moved into a large and beautiful house. Móricz's connections enabled him to obtain special privileges and purchase property. Their first son, Ábrahám, was born in 1797. Sigmund, Eva, Fülöp, and Samuel followed. The family was destined for a blissful, abundant life. Until the war came, and disaster struck this happy family.

The End of Prosperity

Since 1792, France's revolutionary government had engaged in military conflicts with various European nations. The Austrian Empire was their main adversary. In 1809, Austria led a coalition against France in an attempt to avenge several humiliating defeats. With major battles beginning in April, Napoleon achieved quick victories. In May, Napoleon invaded Austria and laid siege to Vienna, the second time Vienna had fallen to the French in four years. An armistice in July led to the Treaty of Schönbrunn, named for the palace where it was signed on October 14, 1809.

Zsigmond wrote, "Napoleon's mighty army reached Austria and Hungary and tormented the citizens there, along with the locals." The wealthy Jewish population was particularly vulnerable. Most Jews were not allowed to own real estate. Stocks and bonds were not yet available. Jewish wealth was tied up in goods, money, gold, and jewelry. General citizens of the Austro-Hungarian Empire thought that all Jews were millionaires. They directed the French soldiers to Jewish homes, which were subsequently robbed.

Rachel was pregnant with Samuel, their fifth child, and not in good health. To protect his family, Móricz buried their gold, silver, jewelry, and all their other valuables before French soldiers arrived in Kittsee. He never told anyone, not even Rachel, the location of their possessions. The French soldiers, coming to this large stately house, decided that they would appropriate it for their own use and demanded all of Móricz's assets.

They did not believe Móricz when he told them that his assets had already been stolen. They tortured him. They dug up the basement down to its foundation, drank all the wine that had been stored there, and ate all the food. They continued to torture Móricz. One day, a drunken soldier got hold of Móricz, yelling and demanding that he turn over his money. When Móricz held firm in his position that he did not have any, another solder hit him over the head with his rifle. Móricz sank into a coma from which he never awoke. Imprisoned in their home, with no medical help, Móricz died a few days later.

Alone

By the time Rachel gave birth to Samuel, the French troops had withdrawn. Everyone wanted to help the family. Large donations poured in from Vienna and Pressburg. Relatives of Rachel's late father-in-law, Eisik, came to help.

Tragedy struck again. Rumors spread about Móricz's hidden treasures. Someone set the house on fire, thinking they would find the hidden treasure that way. The fire burnt part of the attic and roof. No treasure was found, but it made life far more difficult for Rachel and her family. Somewhat later a casket was found under a stall in the barn with one hundred ducats and a few items of silver and jewelry. One hundred ducats was the equivalent of about $200 dollars in 1809, or $5,000 in present day dollars. The remaining treasure hidden by Móricz, was never found.

The donations that had poured in were helpful, but not enough to sustain the family over the long term. Rachel was grateful when Fanny and Nathan von Arnstein, (see **Fanny and Nathan von Arnstein on page 46**) offered to bring Rachel's eldest child, Ábrahám, to Vienna. The Arnsteins put Ábrahám in the care of a foster family, arranged for him to be educated by a surveyor, and paid for all his costs.

Land surveying was a professional occupation in high demand at the turn of the 19th century. New techniques were developed with improvements in surveying instrumentation and technology. With the onset of the Industrial Revolution and the development of cities, roads, and railways, it became more important than ever to have accurate land plot measurements and descriptions. With his brilliant mind and his love of mathematics and geometry, it was the ideal career for him.

Rachel's second son, Sigmund, became an apprentice with the leather dealer Wertheimer. Fülöp, the third son, went to work for the Lewinsky trucking company in Pressburg. Only Eva and Samuel were still at home with Rachel.

Rachel took on needlework to make extra money. As Zsigmond writes, "During the day she and Eva would do the housework and at night, undeterred, they would work to make sure they were able to buy bread." Ábrahám, devoted to his mother and siblings, visited them on his days off. The walk between Vienna and Kittsee took at least twelve hours each way. And Ábrahám made even more sacrifices, going without meals in order to give food to Rachel and his siblings.

Financial Hardship

Life did not get easier for Rachel.

In April 1815, a gigantic volcanic eruption on a small Indonesian island triggered dramatic climate changes. Across Europe, average temperatures fell, harvests withered under never-ending rain, and snow fell in June and July. Between 1816 and 1818, the "year without summer," crop failures, war debts, and the devaluation of money led to hunger and hardship throughout greater Europe. It is hard to imagine how Rachel and her children, already poor, could endure further catastrophe. But more was yet to come.

Emperor Francis II passed a decree that banned Jews from the study of surveying. Ábrahám found himself in desperate circumstances, made worse when his benefactor, Fanny Arnstein, passed away. Ábrahám's brothers earned barely enough money to feed themselves, let alone help the family. Rachel was destitute but managed to endure for eight more years.

Peace

Sometime after 1825, Rachel's love of family, hard work, and resilience were finally rewarded. After Rachel's first grandchild was born to Ábrahám (named Móricz after his deceased grandfather), she moved to Irsa, 150 miles east, close to Budapest. At Rachel's request (she did not want to burden her son's family), Ábrahám rented a small apartment close to his home and furnished it for her. Rachel was happy to leave "the grave of my luck." She was finally able to relax, revel in Ábrahám's growing family, and sharpen her Latin, engaging in stimulating conversations with interesting people. She lived out her life modestly but contented in her cozy apartment.

The date of her death is unknown. There are no death certificates left from this era. In September 2019, András, my sister, and I looked for her tombstone in the Jewish cemetery in Irsa. Neglect and deteriorating limestone made the task impossible. András found a book written by the famous Rabbi, Chaim Kittsee. He had been Rabbi in Alberti-Irsa from 1826 till his death in 1840. In the book, he mentioned that he wrote Rachel's epitaph. But we don't know what he wrote nor when he wrote it.

LEARNING MORE

Fanny and Nathan von Arnstein

The Arnsteins, well-known for their philanthropy, would have been among the wealthy Jewish families that Móricz and Rachel met at the Leitersdorfer home. Nathan Ádám von Arnstein (1748-1838) and his partner Eskeles were financiers to the imperial court (before the rise of the Rothschild house), ennobled members of Viennese society. It was their wives, however, who brought them fame. Sisters Fanny (Arnstein) and Cacilie (Eskeles) were daughters of Daniel Itzig, the master coiner of the Prussian king, Frederick II. The Itzigs were one of the most influential Jewish families in Berlin.

According to her peers, Fanny was an angel-faced "blond Jew" with deep blue eyes. She was educated, bright, an excellent conversationalist, and a trained musician who sang and played the piano skillfully. She fought passionately for the rights and acceptance of Jews. She became close to Joseph II and may have played a role in Joseph's issuing the Edict of Toleration (1782).

The two sisters brought the "intellectual salon" to Vienna, attracting leading composers and musicians (Mozart, Beethoven) and writers (Johann Wolfgang von Goethe, Franz Grillparzer). Famous thinkers of the time (Arthur Schopenhauer) along with aristocrats (Prince Wellington, Lord Nelson) also found their way to their salon and its stimulating exchange of ideas. Fanny's influence was at its height during the Congress of Vienna (1814–1815), the international conference that remade Europe at the end of the Napoleonic Wars. History describes how "the Congress danced" in the exquisite ballrooms of the Arnstein's mansion in Vienna and villa at Schönbrunn.

Fanny tried to persuade the Austrian and Prussian nobles in attendance to grant Jews equal rights, but to no avail. During this time, Fanny imported from Berlin the custom of decorating the Christmas tree, creating a sensation that caught on throughout the empire.

Fanny was a great philanthropist and an ardent Austrian patriot. She organized the nursing of soldiers wounded in the Napoleonic wars. It was most likely she who convinced her husband to help Móricz's family.

Fanny and Nathan von Arnstein.

FAMILY TREE

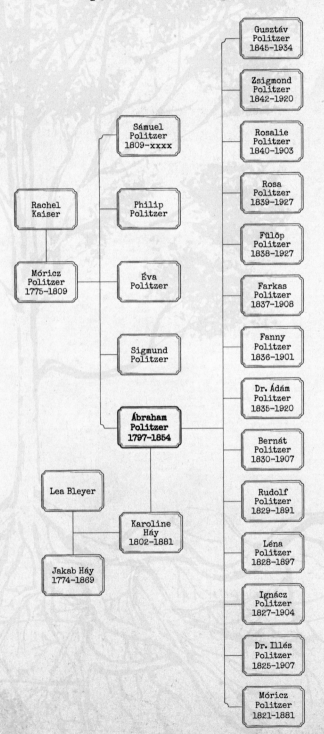

Chapter 5

The Story of Ábrahám

Ábrahám (1797-1854) was Móricz and Rachel's eldest child. He was Zsigmond's father and my great-great-great-great-grandfather (six generations before me). The patriarch of a large family, he instilled in his children values such as love of family, commitment to service and caring for those less fortunate. These values were handed down through the generations to my own family.

A Horrific Day

Zsigmond noted in *Our Family History* that in 1854, November 16th was "the most horrific day in our lives." That was the day that Ábrahám Politzer, age 57, died. His son, Zsigmond wrote, "...without exaggeration, I can truly say that our father was the most perfect, smartest, and best humankind that I have ever met. I've come to know many, many folks during my long life, some very smart, some very wise, some very considerate but only once have I experienced all those characteristics in one single human being: my father."

Death Registry recording Ábrahám's death in 1854. Courtesy of András Gyekiczki.

Ábrahám's funeral, two days later, was a huge event in Alberti and Irsa, as many people from both towns attended. Zsigmond continued, "Not only us, but the poor and needy citizens who needed support or advice had also lost their father, their rock, their wise and kindhearted man to go to."

Beloved

I was humbled when I read Zsigmond's words. It is with great deference that I attempt to tell the story of this beloved man. What I came to learn, I summarize here. This was a man who:

> *Was devoted to his mother, his siblings, his wife, and his fourteen children and, through love, knew happiness and contentment all his life.*
>
> *Showed that hard work, commitment, and persistence, no matter what one's circumstance, could bring abundance in all things, financial and otherwise.*
>
> *Believed in bettering oneself through education, in encouraging his children to be the best they could be, and in rejoicing in their successes small and large.*
>
> *Was steadfast throughout great adversity, being forced to live under treacherous conditions while soldiers took over his home, not once but three times.*
>
> *Defined the word generous, taking in relatives' children and grandchildren to raise as his own, and giving not only financial resources, but also of himself to all – family, friends, and those in need.*

In 1809, the year French soldiers invaded his home and tortured and killed his father, Ábrahám was twelve years old. In those days he would have been considered a man. He was the eldest son and responsible for his family, a responsibility he took seriously.

His father, Dr. Móricz Politzer, instilled in him a curiosity and a love of learning. Like his father, he had a brilliant mind, able to learn easily and quickly. I imagine he was conflicted when Nathan von Arnstein, his benefactor, brought him to Vienna. The allure of learning a new skill using math, which he loved, advancing into the lucrative career of land surveying, and being able to care for his family had to be exciting for this young man — really just a boy. But separating from his mother and siblings after losing his father must have been heart wrenching. He worked hard to become a surveyor. On his days off he walked twelve hours to see his loved ones in Kittsee.

Ábrahám Walks to Hungary

When Emperor Francis II issued a decree banning Jews from studying surveying, Ábrahám's studying was cut short. The decree was in reaction to an uprising in Galicia (now Poland and the Ukraine) where peasants killed landowners and surveyors. Some surveyors had accepted bribes from the wealthy landowners, cheating the poor out of good land. Many of these surveyors were Jewish, as, Zsigmond claimed, "Jews have a good head for arithmetic." The emperor's decree ended the uprising, leaving Ábrahám in a desperate situation.

All Ábrahám's studying had been for naught. His opportunities were diminished. The reactionary politics in the second decade of the 1800s resulted in a return to Jewish restrictions and the limitations on freedoms of past years. Ábrahám had nowhere to turn. After the Congress of Vienna (1814-1815), Fanny and Nathan Arnstein retired to their country estate, worn out from a hectic social life and a debilitating war. In June 1818, Fanny died of a lung ailment. With his benefactors gone, Ábrahám's future seemed bleak.

Ábrahám must have been approaching 20 when he set out on foot to Hungary, as Zsigmond describes, "...with empty pockets, an empty stomach, and believing in God to help him out." He arrived in Pest County, after several days of walking the 175 miles. Pécel, in Pest-Pilis-Solt-Kiskun County (today Pest County), was a growing Jewish community east of current day Budapest. In the second half of the 18th century, the estate owner, Count Ráday, permitted Jews to settle on his estate. Under his patronage, the community grew, and its business owners thrived. Ábrahám was hired as a teacher, a job that paid modestly. He was given a bed at the prayer-leader's house and frugally fed by his students' parents, eating beans for lunch and a piece of bread for dinner six days a week.

He was grateful to have a roof over his head and food to eat, as meager as it was. His heart ached upon receiving letters from his mother and siblings, describing famine and impoverished circumstances. He couldn't have foreseen how his circumstances would change in the next few years.

Uncle and Nephew Unite

One day, Ábrahám received a message from Wolf Politzer. It was a request to come to a meeting place, Landstrasse (now Károly körút) in Pest the following day. Ábrahám knew that Wolf Politzer was his uncle, his father's older brother. He had never met him and knew nothing about him. The message piqued his curiosity, and he went to meet his uncle the following day.

At an early age, Wolf had left the family to apprentice with a merchant in Pressburg. After learning all he could, he set off to build his own agrarian business. He travelled extensively between lower Hungary, Transylvania and Slovenia, areas abundant in agricultural goods but difficult to reach because of the terrible transportation system.

On his journeys, Wolf often met Jakab Háy, another Jewish entrepreneur. They were hard-working, good businessmen with a talent for finding and capitalizing on opportunities. Instead of becoming rivals, they decided to help each other. Or, as Zsigmond described, "...they worked out a deal where one hand washed the other." Ultimately, the friendship became a partnership.

After some time, they both settled in Irsa, a town 25 miles southeast of Pécel. Irsa was one of three communities that had a large and vibrant Jewish population; the other two were old-Buda and Abony. Jakab married Lea, the daughter of the merchant Ruben Bleyer. They had three daughters and a son. When Wolf became engaged, he followed Jakab to Irsa to raise his own family. Jakab and Wolf's partnership turned into a successful wool business.

With the business flourishing, it became essential to hire someone who could write agreements and maintain correspondence with their growing number of wholesalers from the far-reaching areas of the empire. The job required proficiency in writing Yiddish, German and Hungarian, skills difficult to find in lower Hungary. Most Jews only spoke Yiddish and were not well educated.

Joining the Family Business

During his business travels, Wolf was not able to keep in touch with his siblings in Kittsee. He had never met his nieces and nephews. Somehow, he learned that his brother's son had been educated in Vienna and had travelled to Pest to find new opportunities. Perhaps his nephew might be able to fulfill the job of scribe. On market day in Pest, he inquired if someone knew a young man with the name Politzer. Someone Jewish from a nearby town recalled that the teacher in Pécel was named Politzer. Through this circuitous network, Ábrahám received the message from Wolf.

Zsigmond quotes Jakab Háy's description of their historic meeting:

> *The day after we sent the message (to Ábrahám) and sat at lunch, a pale and skinny young man, with his worn-out shoes and a small haversack in his hands entered the room and said he was Aber (Ábrahám) Politzer. He had walked barefoot from Pécel to Pest. Well, this was not the best of entries. Still, we let him have a hearty meal first and, poor guy, he devoured it. After grace was said, Wolf went out with the young man to buy him underwear, clothes, and a pair of boots. Upon return, he made a much better impression, since he was actually a slender and rather handsome person.*

The meeting may have taken place at the Orczy Café or the nearby Jewish Café. During the first half of the 19th century, all civic forums were closed to Jews. Cafés became the places where Jews met, negotiated deals, and carried on financial transactions. The Orczy and Jewish cafés, situated next to the Jewish market, served as the business centers for the Jews of Pest.

Later that evening, as a test, Ábrahám was given the task of leading a prayer for a local Jewish gathering. "His pleasant voice impressed all those present, and he was embraced by the community." Ábrahám passed this preliminary trial; Wolf and Jakab were ready to take a chance on this young man.

Ábrahám sent a farewell letter to the community in Pécel and traveled to Irsa with his uncle and Jakab. Wolf gave him a room in his house. Several days later, Ábrahám went with Wolf to the office in Jakab's house.

Wolf dictated a letter and watched with amazement how efficiently Ábrahám wrote. Wolf and Jakab knew they had found their man. Not only did Ábrahám write fast and legibly, but he also substituted words that enhanced the text.

The Orczy House where Ábrahám met Wolf Politzer and Jakab Háy. Courtesy of the Hungarian Jewish Museum and Archives.

Jewish Community Leader

Ábrahám's reputation grew, as Jakab talked about "this remarkable young man." When Rabbi Zsigmond Bulcher (1860-1941) wrote *The Story of the Jewish Community in Alberti-Irsa* (1909), he mentioned that there was "a pilgrimage to the house of Jakab Háy to look at the smart correspondent whose pen in the hand ran with an admirably insane speed on the paper."

Curious, Jakab's two eldest daughters came to the office to meet him. The eldest daughter, Karoline (nicknamed Golde) and Ábrahám fell in love. At first, they kept it secret, but eventually they wanted to marry. Jakab was smart enough to value character and intelligence over money. Though Ábrahám was poor, Jakab allowed the marriage to proceed. Zsigmond remarked, "His (Jakab's) intuition was correct and he never regretted this decision. He and our father have always had a very strong bond. And Jakab never made important business decisions without consulting his son-in-law, or, as he put it, his best and most loyal child."

Ábrahám and Karoline used her small dowry to open a store. The store prospered and brought moderate wealth to their family. Karoline managed the store and their household, while Ábrahám travelled with Wolf and Jakab on business trips. As Ábrahám was given a share of the profit from these trips, their affluence grew.

Ábrahám became a respected leader in the community. *In The Story of the Jewish Community in Alberti-Irsa*, Rabbi Bulcher wrote, "Ábrahám's wise phrases became like proverbs and were the talk of the town." The Jewish community made Jakab its president and asked Ábrahám to be clerk. To demonstrate their loyalty to the Hungarian nation, the minutes were written in Hungarian, rather than Yiddish. Again, Ábrahám was the best person for the job.

Over the next 24 years Karoline gave birth to sixteen children, of which fourteen survived. The first six children, five boys and one girl, came in rapid procession. The sixth child, Bernát, was born in the middle of the cholera epidemic.

Jakab Háy (1774-1869), my great-great-great-great-great-grandfather.

Cholera

The Asiatic Cholera Pandemic originated in India in 1826 and quickly spread west across trade and military routes. It struck Hungary in 1830-1831 with 250,000 cases and 100,000 deaths, although such statistics are unreliable.

The cholera epidemic interrupted Ábrahám's blissful family life. Pregnant Karoline cried and prayed for her family's health. Her prayers were answered; they were safe. They had moved to the neighboring village of Alberti. The street bordering Alberti and Irsa was turned into a trench. The townsfolk from both sides would meet, keeping a distance of 20 fathoms (40 yards), to inform the other of the latest infections or deaths. "Peasants and citizens armed with pitchforks kept order day and night. It was horrible," Zsigmond reported.

When Karoline gave birth to a healthy baby boy, she named him after the rabbi who had passed away a few days prior. As Zsigmond claims, Bernát lived up to his namesake, with "the demeanor, modesty and religious devotion" of the rabbi. Bernát was my great-great-grandfather. And this was the first thing I learned about the man he was.

The Family Prospers

Ábrahám and Karoline's love of family and generosity knew no bounds. Lea, Jakab's wife, was lost to the epidemic. Jakab remarried and moved to Abony, a town 20 miles away, to be with his father. Karoline took in Jakab's two daughters, Feile and Fogele, and raised them as her own. This did not stop the growing family. The next twelve years, Karoline had eight more pregnancies. Two children died young. Mihaly, at the age of six months, was accidentally smothered in his sleep by his wet nurse. Sami died at age six of scarlet fever. Five boys and three girls survived, bringing the number of children to fourteen. Like so many of that era, they had a large family: fourteen children and two foster children!

In Ábrahám's and Karoline's eyes, every child was precious and treated like a jewel. Though they were Jewish, the boys were sent to secondary school in Pest run by the Piarists (Catholic priests) so they could get the best education available. There is no mention of the four girls attending secondary school. As was the norm for upper class families in the early 19th century, they most likely went to elementary school in Irsa and then were schooled at home. Nevertheless, they were encouraged in all of their pursuits.

No expense was spared if any of the children were ill. When Farkas, the ninth child, turned four and still hadn't spoken, Ábrahám consulted with the famous Professor Stahly in Pest. Miraculously, right before he was to have an operation for a tongue defect, Farkas began to speak. When a scabies epidemic kept all the children home, including Ádám who was sent home from school in Pest, Ábrahám brought Dr. Feuer from Pest who prescribed a salve that a nurse applied to all the children from head to toe. They were quarantined in the farmhouse in the courtyard and made to bathe with warm water every day for two weeks until they were cured. "Our childhood was happy and beautiful. My parents' home was heaven on earth," recalled Zsigmond.

Karoline complained that she never got to see all of her fourteen children together at once. One or another was always missing. Once, the ten sons were all together, so they hired a photographer to have a picture taken.

Reading this, I was reminded of my parents. When we were older and spread across the globe, my mother planned an annual summer weekend together, usually at the family farm, where pictures for the Christmas card would be taken. There is something universal about a parent's desire to see the family together. I understood Karoline's frustration. How András and I wished to find the picture of the ten Politzer brothers together, but we had no such luck.

Philanthropy

Religious life was important to Ábrahám and Karoline's family. They owned two prayer seats at the synagogue. Charity was a serious part of their religious obligation, and the Politzers were generous donors. Two donation books from 1823 and 1832 mention the Politzers many times on the charity lists. (The notes may have been recorded by Ábrahám.) In 1847, a period of terrible inflation, the Jewish community gave grain to the poor regardless of religious affiliation. Ábrahám was listed as the largest donor. He also contributed a substantial amount to the Chevra Kadisha (Jewish burial society).

Donations from the Politzers and Háys were listed in these donation books from the synagogue in Irsa, 1823 and 1832. Courtesy of the Hungarian Jewish Museum and Archives.

The 1848 Revolution

The year 1848 started as others had, with the bright promise of new opportunities, the culmination of hard work and preparation. As Zsigmond recalled, "Our father, due to his great sense of business, had made it to the top. Despite the huge demands of his big family, no one had to suffer. He was able to provide beyond their needs. All the children were well taken care of." (see **Ábrahám's Children on page 65**).

The year had barely begun when numerous political upheavals, called the Springtime of the Peoples, erupted in Sicily (January), France (February) and then spread throughout Europe. (see **Hungarian Revolution of 1848 on page 66**). Only Russia, Spain, and the Scandinavian countries were unaffected. These were populist uprisings against those in power. In the nearly three decades since 1820, there had been numerous instances of such political upheavals, due to a rising working class, the demand for more participation and democracy, an upsurge of nationalism (desire for independent nation-state), and the widespread dissatisfaction with the repressive policies of the monarchies. In 1845-1846, poor grain harvests and depressed economic conditions led to sharply rising food prices, unemployment, and radicalization of the political attitudes of the working class. By 1848, these forces converged and coalitions of reformers, middle class citizens, students and workers rebelled. On March 13, 1848, protesters marched on the Habsburg government.

Ábrahám and Karoline's second oldest child, Illés, was attending medical school in Vienna. They became distraught when they had not heard from Illés for quite some time. With the advent of the riverboat and steam powered trains, news could be delivered in one or two days. They knew the Austrian military had fired on the protesters, innocent citizens and students, and heard about casualties in Vienna, where the demonstrations had begun. They were greatly relieved when Illés' letter finally arrived, announcing that he had joined the Academic Legion, a newly formed military guard composed of citizens, mostly students, to keep the peace.

In April (1848), when Emperor Ferdinand appointed Count Batthyány prime minister of Hungary's new parliamentary government, Ábrahám and his family celebrated, as did many Hungarians. The Politzer home became a center for the festivities in Alberti. The new laws created a modern Magyar (Hungarian) state and included freedom of the press, equality of worship (though no explicit mention of Jewish emancipation), universal equality before the law, and the right to vote for all males over 20 who met property requirements and spoke Hungarian. These rights were worthy of celebration and no blood had been spilled to win them.

Their joy was short-lived. By July, Austrian Imperial forces took back Bohemia and Italy. In October, there was a second revolution launched in Vienna. Illés wanted to return, resolved to fight for the people's new hard-won freedoms. With bad news trickling in every day, Ábrahám would not let him go. It was a wise decision. Austrian Imperial forces together with Croatian forces battered Vienna with heavy artillery fire. By the end of October, Imperial troops overtook Vienna, leaving over 2,000 revolutionaries, mostly workers and students, dead.

Over the next few months Austrian successes came rapidly and by January the Imperial royal army occupied Pest and Buda. It must have been during this time that many of the stores in Pest were shuttered, including the haberdashery where Bernát worked. Bernát returned to Alberti-Irsa and fought with the Hungarian army.

Home Invasion

Fighting broke out in Szolnok, a town 65 miles southeast of Budapest on the banks of the Tisza River. As the troops marched to Szolnok, they passed through Alberti-Irsa. It was a particularly cold winter, as Zsigmond recalls, "With deep felt empathy as we watched the tired infantry drag themselves through the snow past our house. Especially sad was to see the Italian Ceccopieri regiment; their once blue uniforms now in rags, dirty and wet, shivering young men. Their boots were nearly shredded. And yet, these brave young souls stood by the beloved Hungarian flag. They gratefully took everything offered to them along the way: food, water, bread, and wine." Hussars (the Hungarian light cavalry regiments) brought up the rear.

Following the Hussars, but keeping their distance from them, was the Austrian regiment. With their arrival, life changed for the Politzer family. Austrian officers took over their home. As Zsigmond wrote, "It was a horrible time... They took over our 'Parade Room' in the front part of the house and confiscated the rest of the house. We were ordered around and so help us God when we did not obey. Our parents and the children had to make do with two small rooms for all of us."

Throughout the next eight to twelve weeks, with armies trudging back and forth to the fighting in Szolnok, the Politzer house was in great danger, as armies loyal to the monarchy invaded their home.

The fear and stress Ábrahám would have experienced must have been unimaginable. He had been only twelve when the French soldiers took over his home and murdered his father. Almost 40 years later, he feared that history would be repeated.

The soldiers, particularly the Croatian soldiers, stole everything in sight. Ábrahám knew to hide their valuable items, as his father had. The soldiers were careless. Zsigmond recounted how one rainy night, Austrian soldiers took over Ábrahám and Karoline's bedroom. Drenched to the skin, they dumped wet gunpowder out on a table. It was only luck that a spark from the nearby candle didn't ignite the gunpowder and blow up the house.

The tide turned when the Hungarian army reorganized. In what was known as the Spring campaign of 1849, a series of Hungarian victories forced the Austrians to retreat. The Politzer house was freed from intruders for a short time, as were all of Alberti and Irsa. Though there was no active fighting in the town, the soldiers looted and burned buildings. Many of the town records were destroyed, including most of the birth and death certificates.

At the beginning of April, days before Easter, a loud blast occurred, sending everyone to the floor. They were relieved to find that it was not from local fighting. The blast had come from a battle at Tápióbicske, 10 miles northeast of Alberti-Irsa. By nighttime, the Hungarians were victorious there.

The next day brought fear and anxiety to Ábrahám and Karoline, instead of a victory celebration. Their two sons, Ádám (13 years old) and Fülöp (10 years old), snuck out of the house to visit the site of the battle. Exhausted from the four-hour walk, the boys were shocked to see the battlefield with so many dead soldiers. Fortuitously, a neighbor recognized the young boys and took them home in his wagon. Ábrahám and Karoline, beside themselves with worry, gave them their first (and only) harsh punishment, according to Zsigmond, though he did not specify what the punishment was.

By May of 1849, the Hungarian army pushed the Imperial army back towards Pest and Buda, culminating in the Siege of Buda. The population of Pest fled to nearby towns. Despite their lack of room, the Politzers took in six members of the Kunewalder family. The father, Zsigmond Kunewalder, was an army medic and may have been a colleague of Illés. When the siege ended on May 21st with the Hungarian capture of the castle and the death of General Hentzi, the family of six returned to their home.

After the Siege of Buda, the Austrian-Russian army marched south, passing Alberti-Irsa on their way. Once again, the Politzer home was taken over by soldiers. This time, it was primarily Russian soldiers. Zsigmond recalled, "... their manners were much better than that of the Austrians. Even common Cossacks were playing with the children and teaching them Russian songs. The officers were considerate and modest."

The soldiers didn't stay long, as the fighting moved east into what is now present-day Romania. The heroic Hungarian efforts were hopeless against the Russian and Austrian forces. Sándor Petőfi, the poet and spiritual leader of the war, was killed in battle. Less than two weeks later, on August 9th, the Hungarians lost at the Battle of Temesvár. Hungarians formally declared their surrender on August 13, 1849.

Battle Locations Near Albertirsa, 1849

An Uneasy Peace

Retribution followed surrender. Austrian General Haynau, nicknamed "the hangman of Arad," was appointed to restore order. Known for his brutality, he ordered the whipping of women suspected of sympathizing with the insurgents, hanged over 100 people including thirteen rebel generals, and authorized vicious reprisal attacks in a campaign of terror.

Jakab Háy, Ábrahám's father-in-law, was not spared. Seventy-five years old at the time, he spent several weeks in the prison of Cegléd for his support of the opposition. When the leader of the Hungarian freedom fighters came to Abony, Jakab had donated his valuable copper, zinc, and silverware to finance their efforts. He even donated items like candlesticks and kiddush cups that he used for religious purposes. Dr. Béla Vajda, Rabbi of Abony, wrote in the *History of the Jews in Abony* (1896), "This is how this holy, grey-haired man demonstrated that those who contribute to religious causes are always ready for any sacrifice for their homeland."

Hungarian Jews had given generously to the Hungarian army, demonstrating their loyalty to Hungary despite anti-Jewish demonstrations when Hungary's independent government was announced in April 1848. The response to Jewish loyalty: harsh reprisals against Jewish citizens. It is estimated that over 1,000 Jewish veterans emigrated to America and volunteered for the Union Army during the Civil War rather than endure Haynau's revenge. Haynau ordered the Jewish community to pay 2.3 million gulden in war reparations (approximately $35 million today.)

Ábrahám and Karoline, prominent Jewish Hungarians in the community, feared for themselves and for their children. German replaced Latin and Hungarian as the official language, and German-speaking administrators were put in place. As Zsigmond described, "Foreign civil servants, mostly Czechs, who didn't speak our language, came and ran the land with the utmost harshness." This absolutist regime was aimed at centralizing the monarchy and eliminating all vestiges of Hungarian autonomy. It wouldn't be until the Austro-Hungarian Compromise of 1867, which established the Dual Monarchy, that Hungary would once again have an independent government.

A Brutal Robbery

In 1853 the Politzer home was robbed and Ábrahám and Karoline attacked. A bricklayer, familiar with the house after many repairs, opened the bedroom closet where they'd hidden money. When Karoline woke up and screamed his name, he hit her over the head, knocking her out. Meanwhile, his accomplice went after Ábrahám with an axe.

Zsigmond, 11 years old, suffering from a painful toothache, had fallen asleep in his father's bed. He woke up and pulled the thick blanket over his father, softening the blow from the robber. The bed was covered in blood. The robbers thought both Ábrahám and Karoline were dead. Ábrahám snuck out of the room and made noises in the hallway, waking his sons and servants. They stormed into the room to help. The robbers fled.

Luckily, Illés happened to be home at the time. With his training and war experience, he immediately knew what needed to be done for his parents. Ábrahám's little finger remained crooked; the axe had cut the ligaments when he used his hand to block the blow to his head. Karoline recovered with a small scar on her forehead as a souvenir of that terrible night.

An Untimely Death

Unfortunately, Illés was not there when, a year later, in November 1854, Ábrahám, returning from a business trip in Pest, complained of abdominal pain. The doctor diagnosed intestinal twisting. Appendicitis was yet to be understood. Within the day, before many of his children and another doctor arrived, Ábrahám died, leaving behind his wife and eight of his fourteen children who were still living at home. He had known only four of his fifty-six grandchildren. Zsigmond lamented, "Days and weeks of extreme sadness filled our orphaned home."

Four years later, Karoline moved to Pest to be close to her children and grandchildren. She never returned to Alberti-Irsa, where "she spent so many happy years, had good neighbors, raised her children, and lived a good life with Ábrahám." For the rest of her 23 years, she remained homesick for her home in Alberti-Irsa.

LEARNING MORE

Ábrahám's Children

Ábrahám's oldest son, Móricz (named for his grandfather), was in the wool business. He married, settled in Kecskemét (30 miles south), and started a family of his own. Illés, the second oldest, was in the last year of his medical studies in Vienna, looking forward to a promising career following in his grandfather Móricz's footsteps. Ignácz, the third son, who, according to Zsigmond had a great sense of humor, was traveling throughout the empire, as part of a gingerbread baking apprenticeship. Ignácz was "well-resourced by our father with all the necessities he'd need along his travels." Rudolf, the fifth child, started in his father's business and then moved to Abony to start his own. Bernát moved to Pest to work for the renowned haberdashery company Jakab Hirsch and Sons. Ádám was in Pest in secondary school. Except for Gustáv, who was only two years old, the other boys (Farkas, Fülöp and Zsigmond) attended elementary school in Alberti.

The four girls were also living at home. Lena, the fourth child and oldest daughter, was nineteen at the time. "Good hearted with a golden character," according to Zsigmond, she helped her mother with the younger children. Fanny, Rosa, and Rosalie were also of elementary school age and most likely attended the girl's school in Alberti.

Hungarian Revolution of 1848

The Hungarian Revolution was part of a European-wide uprising triggered by nationalism (a patriotic desire for independence), economic instability, and liberal ideas (such as freedom and equal rights) unleashed among intellectuals after the Napoleonic War. The idea of nationalism for Hungary was complicated since Hungary included many different ethnic groups with different loyalties, including Slavs, Croats, Serbs, Romanians and Slovenes. The rebellion in Hungary coincided with rebellions in Vienna, Italy, and Bohemia (Czech Republic). Austria did not have the military resources to extinguish four simultaneous rebellions.

Emperor Ferdinand Yields to Calls for Freedom and Hungary Independence

On March 3, 1848, Lajos Kossuth, a lawyer, publisher of the magazine Pesti Hírlap, a member of the Hungarian Diet in Pressburg (Bratislava), and a talented orator, delivered a fiery speech before the Hungarian legislative body in which he demanded liberal reforms, a constitution for the Habsburg monarchy, and establishment of a responsible ministry in Hungary.

Students in Vienna, emboldened by the success of the Paris Revolution and Kossuth's speech, ten days later presented Emperor Ferdinand with a petition demanding a constitution and freedom of the press. The next day, thousands gathered before the House of Estates for the opening session of the legislature in Vienna, demanding freedom, transparency, and representation for Austrian citizens. Soldiers were ordered to open fire on the demonstrators.

The situation soon grew out of control – excise houses were burned, shops looted, and factories destroyed. Two days of violence ensued. Eventually, the civic guard joined the demonstrators and delivered an ultimatum demanding Chancellor Metternich's dismissal, the withdrawal of troops in the city, and arming of the students. On March 15th, the Habsburg monarchy acceded to the demands and an "Academic Legion" (similar to a national guard) was established to keep the peace.

When news of the events in Vienna reached Pest, demonstrations broke out. The famed poet, Sándor Petőfi, read twelve demands and recited a poem, "The National Song," to a crowd that swelled into the thousands. They began to march around the city, seizing the presses, liberating political prisoners, and declaring the end of Austrian rule. But not all Hungarians were in favor of civil rights for all, as antisemitism simmered beneath the surface. Anti-Jewish demonstrations broke out at the same time in Pest.

Following the demonstrations, a Hungarian delegation travelled to Vienna to present the demands to Emperor Ferdinand. It took only a day for Ferdinand to concede. Count Lajos Batthyány, a member of the Hungarian Diet and leader of the opposition, returned to Pest as Prime Minister of the new Hungarian government.

Hungary Fights to Keep New Freedoms

The new freedoms would not last long. Counterrevolutions swept the land within the year. Deaths were estimated in the tens of thousands, although such statistics were not well kept. By June and July of 1848, Austrian Imperial forces had already taken back Bohemia (Prague Uprising) and Italy (Milan and Lombardy).

In September, provoked by Kossuth's movement to make Magyar the official language of Hungary, the Croatians, loyal to Austria, invaded Hungary. After repulsing the Croatian forces, a Hungarian army crossed the border into Austria. A second revolution had broken out in Vienna on October 6th and the Hungarians tried to help the revolutionaries. Austrian Imperial forces together with Croatian forces bombarded Vienna and crushed the revolt.

By end of October, the Hungarian government, now lead by Kossuth, was able to muster an army of 100,000, including two Italian battalions and nine Hussar (Hungarian light cavalry) regiments. The majority of Hungarian Jews supported Kossuth, despite anti-Jewish sentiment. Over 20,000 Jews were recruited into the Hungarian army. Jews played an important part in provisioning and equipping the army as well as serving as soldiers, army medics, and surgeons. All resources were critical, as Hungary's war raged on three fronts: fighting Croatian troops to the south, Romanians to the east, and Austrians to the west.

In early December, Emperor Ferdinand abdicated in favor of his nephew, Franz Joseph, who was no longer bound by the promises made in April by his predecessor. Franz Joseph refused to recognize the Hungarian government and ordered his army to attack Hungary. Austrian successes came rapidly and by January the imperial royal army occupied Pest and Buda. The Hungarian government fled to Debrecen.

That winter, the Hungarian army reorganized and launched a full scale counter-attack, called the Spring campaign, against the Austrian army. They achieved a series of victories, and for a time it looked like the tide would turn.

The Siege of Buda

In May 1849, the Austrian army, pushed back by several Hungarian victories, retreated to Pest and Buda, where they controlled the Buda castle. As the Hungarian army approached and laid siege to Buda, General Hentzi of the Imperial army fired upon Pest with explosive and incendiary projectiles. The bombardment started May 4th and continued every day until the end of the siege, resulting in the destruction of many beautiful neoclassical buildings on the shores of the Danube.

The attack on civilians and civilian buildings was contrary to the rules of war and General Hentzi was condemned for his brutality. The population of Pest fled to nearby towns. The siege ended on May 21st with the Hungarian capture of the castle and the death of General Hentzi. On the very day of the end of the siege, Emperor Franz Joseph signed an agreement with Tsar Nicholas of Russia to send troops to crush the revolution.

Hungarians Surrender to the Russians

The Russians surprised everyone with the strength of their response, sending more than 200,000 soldiers to fight with the Austrian troops. Together they overwhelmed the Hungarians. On August 13, 1849, after several bitter defeats, the Hungarians surrendered to the Russians at Világos (now Şiria, Romania). Surrendering to the Russians rather than to the Austrians was their last gesture of defiance, implying that the Hungarians had failed only because of Russian intervention.

Defeat was followed by brutal retaliation against the Hungarians, led by Austrian General Haynau. General Haynau swore to set an example for all of Europe for how rebels should be treated. Count Batthyány, Hungary's prime minister, was executed by firing squad. On Haynau's orders, more than 100 people were executed, 1,200 Imperial officers fighting on the Hungarian side were sentenced to imprisonment, and an additional 40,000 to 50,000 officers and soldiers were conscripted into the Imperial army.

FAMILY TREE

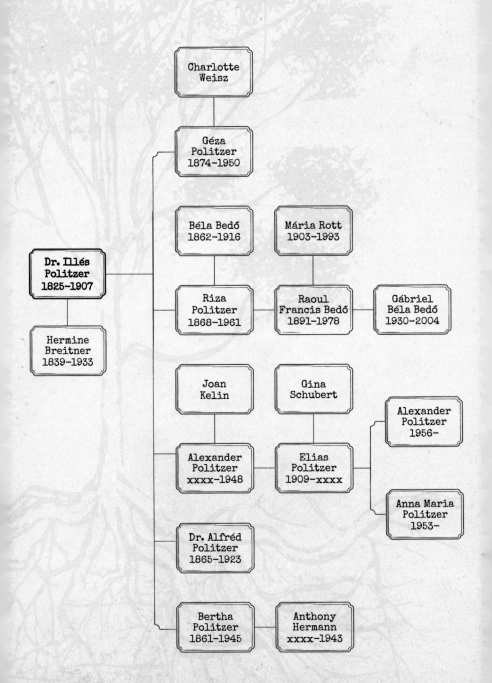

Chapter 6

Illés Politzer

Illés (1825-1907) was the second oldest of Ábrahám and Karoline's children. He was Zsigmond's older brother, and he was my great-great-great-uncle (five generations before me). A freedom fighter in the Hungarian Civic Revolution and War of Independence of 1848-1849, he was admired for his courage, compassion, and humility.

Following His Grandfather

In *Our Family History*, Zsigmond wrote that his parents, Ábrahám and Karoline, considered Illés, their second son, to be their most intelligent child. Like his father and grandfather before him, he was quick, smart, and loved to learn.

From the time he was young, his parents expected he would become a doctor, like his grandfather Móricz. He finished among the top students in the Piarist's School in Pest (the equivalent of high school). In 1847, he enrolled in medical school in Vienna, from which he also graduated at the top with *valde bene* (the highest possible grade).

The Vienna Academic Legion

Illés was in his first year of medical school when the Springtime of the Peoples erupted. On March 13, 1848, several thousand university students, together with reformers, middle class citizens, and workers, marched on the House of Estates for the opening legislature of Vienna, and then went on to the Hofburg, Vienna's castle where the Austrian ministers were meeting. The demonstrators demanded reform for the whole of the Austro-Hungarian empire. They repeatedly chanted, "Down with Metternich." Metternich, chancellor of Austria, had become a symbol of harsh oppression.

We don't know if Illés joined the throngs of protesters that day. The military had been ordered to disperse the mobs, violence broke out, and there were many fatal casualties. Days later, when Illés finally wrote to his parents that he was safe, his family was greatly relieved.

Illés wrote that he had joined the Academic Legion. The Habsburg monarchy had acceded to the demonstrators' demands; Metternich resigned, the Imperial troops withdrew, and an "Academic Legion" (similar to a national guard) was formed to keep the peace.

In June, Illés came home for summer vacation, "dressed in his blue uniform, his tunic buttoned way up to his neck, sword on his side, and the crooked uniform hat on his head." His family was impressed with his newly found responsibility, enthralled with his stories, and happy to have him home. As Zsigmond described, "Being mother's favorite child, it was always a great celebration for all of us when special meals were prepared by mother for her favorite son."

Illés' uniform got little use after his return home. In July and August, the Austrian military started to take back all they had lost, resulting in a second revolution in Vienna in October. Illés wanted to go back to Vienna, to begin his school year and to fight for the people's new hard-won freedoms. His parents would not let him go. They may have saved his life, as thousands of demonstrators, mostly students, died at the hands of Austrian Imperial forces. Its leaders were executed.

The Academic Legion, Vienna. Illés served in the Academic Legion in the spring of 1848. Courtesy of the Austrian National Library.

Joining the Hungarian Revolution of 1848

Illés was prohibited from returning to Vienna to continue his medical studies, but he would not sit idly by. András discovered a document dated January 20, 1849, in which Lázár Mészáros, Minister of Defense, appointed Illés military doctor of the military hospital in Nagyvárad (Oradea, Romania), 123 miles east of Alberti-Irsa.

During those initial winter months, the Hungarians suffered many losses at the hands of the Austrian imperial forces. Illés had to learn quickly, having to operate on the many hundreds of wounded soldiers. I imagine that this experience was better than any medical school training.

In June, Illés contracted typhus fever. He recovered under the care of Dr. Frederick Grosz, a well-known and highly respected (and first Jewish) ophthalmologist. His family was greatly relieved.

In the summer of 1849, the Hungarian army was overwhelmed by Austrian forces that had been reinforced by Russian troops. Several bitter defeats ensued. Illés witnessed the last defeat at the battle of Temesvár (now Timișoara, Romania) on August 9, 1849. Luckily, he was able to retreat, escaping with nearly half the Hungarian army. Those who surrendered were either executed, imprisoned, or drafted into the Imperial army.

Escaping Execution

The victorious Austrian government, under the leadership of General Haynau (known as "the hangman of Arad"), launched a punitive campaign against not only the Hungarian revolutionaries but also their sympathizers, including women, children, and the elderly. "The brutal Haynau agents, detectives, and informers searched and hunted down Hungarians who were then put on trial," Zsigmond recounted.

Illés went into hiding for two and a half months until he was summoned to appear in court. Pál Kelemen, the registrar of Alberti, intervened. In a document dated October 30, 1849, he stated clearly that Illés was not active in the Hungarian Revolution and therefore should be permitted to continue his medical studies. It was an act of courage and compassion. Had his lie been discovered, he would have been executed. It enabled Illés to return to Vienna.

A Rocky Start

Illés finished medical school in 1851. Before he could receive his diploma of surgery, Pál Kelemen had to testify again that Illés had played no part in the Revolution.

After medical school, Illés continued two years of post-doctoral studies in Vienna, under the tutelage of Dr. Franz Schuh, a famous surgeon. He returned to Hungary in 1853 to build his medical practice and to be close to his family. But with the Draconian laws imposed by Austrian Emperor Franz Joseph, life in Hungary was difficult. Ruthless authorities still persecuted any revolutionaries.

Illés moved to a small town, Hajós, 88 miles south of Alberti-Irsa, where he opened an office. During the week he performed complicated surgeries, the kind that "other doctors did not feel comfortable performing." On the weekend he had to patch up farmers who had been seriously injured after silly drunken fights. Zsigmond wrote, "It was a hard time for him." He felt isolated, far from his family and cultural activities. He also felt the stress of the Austrian oppression, and along with other Hungarians, passively resisted the harsh local administrators and the enforcement of the German language.

The following year, 1854, was a year of highs and lows for Illés. A high: his younger brother Ádám chose to follow in his footsteps and enter the medical profession. A low: his father died suddenly, before Illés could get home to see him.

A Humble Doctor Devoted to Family

We don't know when Illés transferred to Pest, probably in the late 1850s. (Buda and Pest were still separate towns.) But there, he was introduced to and fell in love with Hermine Breitner, daughter of a crop trader and real-estate owner (a sign of wealth and prestige as few Jews owned houses at that time). Jewish marriages required official approval from the Imperial courts. It took months for royal officials to respond to Illés' request. Finally in 1860, Illés, 35 years old, married Hermine, 21 years old. Over the next ten years, the couple had five children: three boys and two girls.

It was most likely after the 1868 Emancipation Act, which gave Jews civic and political rights, that Illés settled his family in a rented flat on Sas utca in inner-city Pest. Fifty years earlier, when his father, Ábrahám, first came to Pest, this part of the city was surrounded by walls and Jews would have needed a special permit to enter. Illés set up his medical office and examination room in his home, a common practice in those days.

Illés was hardworking and prudent, but family was his priority. Zsigmond wrote that he and Hermine created a joyful, loving home. Parents and all five children were happy and healthy.

Illés and Hermine, circa 1885.

Illés demonstrated his love by passing his possessions down to his off-spring. "I enjoyed least the fruits of my humble possessions acquired over a lifetime of hard and honorable work. It will give me pleasant comfort to know that I will be able to leave those for my descendants to enjoy. My honorable work and frugal lifestyle should always serve as a model for them," Illés wrote in his will.

Although Illés became a well-known, highly respected doctor, he was unpretentious. He lived a comfortable life, but he never purchased his home. Instead, he invested in two prayer seats in the Dohány Synagogue. When he purchased them, they were not only expensive, but prestigious and in high demand. They cost as much or more than a house. Religion was more important to him than creature comforts. His other assets were the crypt No 35 for eight people in the Jewish cemetery on Kozma Street. He wrote, "... knowing that after my death my family and I will be able to rest in eternal peace in a shared place has been really reassuring for me."

Illés died on January 1, 1907, at age 82. Hermine, 14 years younger than her husband, lived another 26 years. She was 94 when she died in 1933. Of their five children, three are buried in the crypt: their oldest son Albert, their youngest son Géza, and their daughter Riza and her husband Béla Bedő. We don't know where their daughter Bertha Herrmann nor their son Alexander are buried.

Illés Politzer Family Tombstone: Crypt No 35 (R) at the Kozma Street Cemetery, Budapest, Hungary. Photo: Levente Tóth, 2022.

LEARNING MORE

Painting: A Bond Shared by Brothers

After much sleuthing, András learned that the Semmelweis Medical History Library and Museum had in their collection several of Illés' papers. It was where he found Illés' will. He also found a self-portrait.

The portrait surprised us. We knew that Ádám was a talented painter (see **Chapter 7**), and Zsigmond wrote in *Our Family History* about his own love of painting. But we knew nothing about Illés' artistic talent. I wondered if Illés had influenced his brothers' love of art.

In that portrait, I saw a serious, young man. Only twenty-five years old in this self-portrait, he had already experienced war, escaped execution, and returned to his medical studies in Vienna. He was ready to settle down into a new, simple, and peaceful life. If only this painting could talk.

There is no evidence that he painted other paintings. This self-portrait was important to him. In his will, he left it to Géza, his youngest son and favorite child.

Illés passed on his love of art to at least three of his children. Their stories are told in Chapter 10.

Illés self-portrait, dated 1850. Courtesy of Semmelweis University Library.

FAMILY TREE

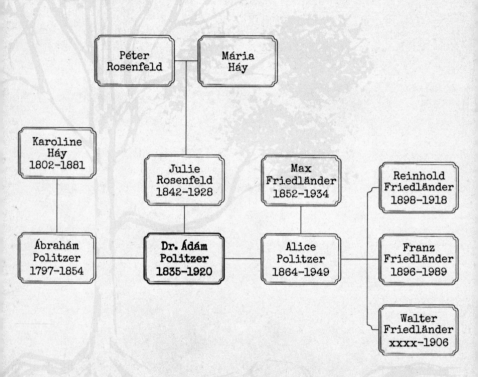

Chapter 7

Ádám Politzer

Ádám Politzer (1835-1920) was the seventh of Ábrahám and Karoline's fourteen children. He was Zsigmond's older and favorite brother, and he was my great-great-great-uncle (five generations before me).

Hints of Family History

During my older brother's second year at medical school, he announced to my parents that he wanted to specialize in ear-nose-and-throat medicine. In response, my mother told him, "Your great-great uncle, Ádám Politzer, was a famous otolaryngologist who lived in Vienna and treated the Emperor Franz Josef and Tsar Nicolas II."

He was of a generation long gone before she met my father. With no mention of Ádám Politzer's religious affiliation, such stories were safe, never hinting of our Jewish ancestry. My mother spoke of him in the 1970s, years before internet searches. A self-absorbed teenager, I didn't think much more about this. I was not interested in going to the library to dig deeper.

When I began to research my family history in 2016, Ádám Politzer was a good starting point. Because he was famous, information about him would be more accessible. A Google search yielded more than 100 entries, including links to numerous books and articles written by and about him, and his own Wikipedia page.

I found the Politzer Society for Otologic Surgery and Science, an active society with annual meetings and awards. I learned about Albert Mudry, a current professor of otolaryngology in Lausanne, Switzerland, and a leading historian in otology, who wrote the definitive book on Ádám Politzer. According to the introduction, the book represents Mudry's "*Magnum Opus*: It is the product of many years of diligent investigative research in libraries and archives supplemented by original material gleaned from Politzer family sources."

After I read that Dr. Mudry owned material from family sources, I emailed him with the subject line, "A request from Ádám Politzer's great-great-great-niece." At the time, I wasn't sure that was the truth. In his reply, less than 24 hours later, he offered to share his sources, but suggested that everything he had was referenced in his book. He apologized that little family information was known because historical documents related to Ádám's Jewish origins were most likely destroyed in World War II.

When I received the box rescued from the fire in my parents' home, I found the book that contained our family tree. I hadn't lied to Dr. Mudry. I really was Ádám Politzer's great-great-great-niece. Among the pictures found in the box was one of Ádám sitting on the balcony of my great-grand-mother Margit's home in Budapest.

According to Dr. Mudry, Ádám had also written an autobiography. Dr. Mudry, and later András (my dedicated researcher in Budapest), pursued every possible path to find this document, but to no avail. Only the first page was found (currently in the Vienna Institute of the History of Medicine). In that first page, Ádám briefly described the lives of Eisik and that of Móricz and Rachel. They were consistent with Zsigmond's stories in *Our Family History*.

A Medical Career

In *Our Family History*, Zsigmond wrote, "My happiest days were when Ádám was home for vacation. I loved him to the point of adoration. I just loved listening to his stories about school." The two brothers, seven years apart, remained close throughout their lives. Beyond a mutual admiration, they shared a deep love of family, a pioneering spirit, artistic talent, and a passion for art collecting.

After primary school in Alberti-Irsa, Ádám attended Catholic boarding school, first in Kecskemét (30 miles south of Ádám's home in Alberti-Irsa) and then in Pest. It was not unusual within the Habsburg monarchy of that time for Jewish boys to attend a Christian run gymnasium, the equivalent

Ádám Politzer on the balcony of my great-grandmother Margit's home on Teréz körút, Budapest, circa 1902.

of high school. The Piarist schools (run by Catholic priests) were preferred by Jews because of the excellence of their instruction. Jewish boys often represented up to 60% of all students, even though Jewish parents had to pay three times the tuition. It was a worthwhile investment in the future. Education enabled many of the empire's Jews to enter the professional middle classes. Jewish parents readily paid the price if they could.

After graduating from secondary school, Ádám considered becoming an artist but eventually chose to pursue a medical career. He may have been influenced by his relatives and teachers. His father, Ábrahám, often regaled Ádám and his siblings with stories of their grandfather, Dr. Móricz Politzer, "the pride of the family" and "the most famous doctor in the neighborhood" (Kittsee). An honest, compassionate, impressive man, Móricz was held up as a role model. It is easy to imagine that Ádám wanted to follow in his grandfather's footsteps.

In 1854, Ádám began his medical studies in Pest. A few months later, his father died. I wondered if Illés became a stronger influence in Ádám's life after Ábrahám's death. After two semesters, Ádám transferred to the University in Vienna, Illés' alma mater. Ádám greatly admired Illés, ten years his senior, and they too stayed close throughout their lives.

At the time there was no systematic course of study for medicine. Students had ample freedom to choose their courses and, most importantly, their teachers. Ádám chose well, taking classes from professors who were at the forefront of medical innovation at the Viennese University. A scientific revolution was underway, enabled by technical developments such as the modern microscope and advances in physiology, anatomy, pathology, and histology. Ádám was well trained to recognize the importance of empirical facts and the value of examination.

Ádám excelled in his studies. The depth and breadth of his knowledge was revealed in eleven articles he published in *Orvosi Hetilap*, the medical journal of Hungary. These were published when he was still a student, an unusual feat at the time. On November 29, 1859, he obtained the highest overall grade possible, *valde bene*. He received the titles of Doctor in Medicine, Doctor in Surgery, and Master of Obstetrics.

Otology Pioneer

Johann von Oppolzer, one of Ádám's renowned university professors, had taken great interest in Ádám. Upon graduation, Oppolzer suggested that Ádám consider specializing in otology (the study of the ear and its diseases), an emerging field. Dr. Oppolzer and Ádám's other professors gave him excellent letters of recommendation with which he secured apprenticeships with the best experts in the field.

His first year was spent as a research assistant to Dr. Carl Ludwig, one of the greatest physiologists of the 19th century. In Ludwig's lab, Ádám developed a medical procedure, known as politzerization, to open the Eustachian tube and equalize pressure in the sinuses. He published his findings in 1861, and in 1863 introduced a medical device for performing the procedure, known as the Politzer bag for which he received international acclaim. Throughout his career, he continuously modified and improved the device, and it is still in use today.

His post-graduate training took him to Würzburg, Heidelberg, Paris, and London. For two years, he worked with distinguished scientists who studied the physiology and pathology of hearing. Medical research remained important to Ádám throughout his career.

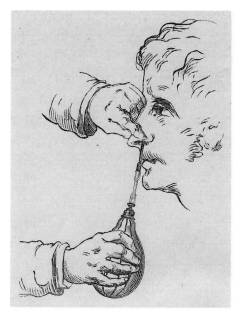

Ádám's illustration of his invention, the Politzer Bag. From *Lehrbuch der Ohrenheilkunde* (Text Book of Ear Medicine), 1878. Courtesy of Dr. Albert Mudry.

When Ádám returned to Vienna in 1862, his former professor, Dr. Oppolzer, gave him a small room to set up his medical practice at the Vienna General Hospital. He was also appointed dozent (lecturer) in otology at the university. Only four students enrolled in his first course.

In 1864, Ádám persuaded the mayor of Vienna to allow him to treat indigent patients with ear problems at the Charity Hospital. Several years later Ádám was asked to treat patients in the city's nursing homes. This gave Ádám a huge patient population to study. One colleague said of him: "He is the most humane physician, who treats the highest and the lowest with the same attention, the same care, and the same concern." Ádám assembled his learnings in a textbook, published in 1865. It laid the foundation for the classification and clinical diagnosis of ear diseases.

Husband and Father

Sometime after he returned to Vienna from his doctoral studies abroad, Ádám married Julie Rosenfeld. How they met remains a mystery. They married in 1862 or 1863. In 1863, Ádám was 28 years old and Julie 21. I found it curious that Zsigmond omitted any mention of Ádám's family in *Our Family History*, given that Ádám was his favorite brother. I presume it was because Ádám had written his own autobiography.

In 1864, Julie gave birth to Alice, their one and only child. We know little about her, other than she was a talented pianist. Most women from well-to-do families learned to play the piano or sing, primarily to improve their marriage opportunities and provide entertainment. But Alice must have been far more serious than that. Her teacher was the famous Johannes Brahms (1833-1897), Director of the Society of Friends of the Music in Vienna. He was particular about the students he would take on, which included such famous names as Antonín Dvořák. Alice would have had to demonstrate significant skill for Brahms to have her as a student.

Mudry wrote in his book that he suspected Brahms may have introduced Alice to her future husband, Max Friedländer. Brahms was close friends with Max, a musicologist from Berlin who often visited Brahms in Vienna. Alice and Max were married sometime in the early 1890s. They moved to Berlin and raised three sons: Walter, Franz, and Reinhold.

Ádám was particularly fond of his three grandsons.

The Father of Otology

Ádám's reputation grew as otology was becoming a recognized field. In 1871, the University named him Extraordinary Professor of Otology (the second level of teaching) together with a colleague named Joseph Gruber. Two years later, the Minister of Education agreed to set up a proper otology clinic, with Ádám and Joseph Gruber as department heads. It was the first otology clinic in the world. It had 20 beds: twelve for men, allotted to Joseph Gruber, and eight for women, allotted to Ádám. Their resources were limited: inadequate equipment, an outpatient clinic held in a small room, one operating room, and one lecture room. But they managed to see 15,000 patients per year and perform 400 operations.

Over time, a great rivalry developed between Ádám and Joseph Gruber. Ádám was demanding in his work and aggressively argued with those who disagreed with him. Their enmity, which lasted throughout their careers, was often hostile and malicious. Nevertheless, the clinic was Ádám's pride and joy.

Ádám's second textbook, published in 1878, became the definitive textbook of the ear in the 19th and 20th century. It contained 878 pages and 258 illustrations, all drawn by Ádám. He was a creative trailblazer, using his artistic gifts to enhance medical knowledge of the ear. He published five more editions until the last one in 1908.

As Ádám's reputation grew, he was summoned abroad in his capacity as a physician and lecturer. (see **Ádám Politzer at the Centennial Exhibition of 1876 in Philadelphia on page 96**) In our family tree book, Gábor Virány (my uncle) had written that Ádám traveled to Russia to treat the Tsar. András could not verify this, but he did find evidence that Ádám treated King Leopold of Belgium. András found numerous articles describing Ádám's travels. His fame was such that his arrival in a city was announced in the local newspapers.

Ádám was proud of his teaching. He was an enormously popular professor. Teaching in six languages (English, German, French, Hungarian, Italian, and Spanish), he taught over 7,000 students from abroad. His students included the leading otologists of their time, including Róbert Bárány who received the Nobel Prize for Medicine in 1914.

Burton Alexander Randall (1858-1932), an American student who studied with Ádám in 1883, described his teaching technique in the following way, "Politzer would examine each patient, then create a small sketch of what he found and attach this to the patient's shoulder. He would then provide an impromptu lecture on the condition, its diagnosis and treatment, and refer to the pictures mounted on the walls of the clinic or the specimens in his collection."

In 1896, Ádám was awarded the highest level of teaching. This appointment came late because otology was not recognized as an independent medical specialty until the 1890s.

Diseases of the ear grew more prevalent as industrialization and urbanization created damaging noise pollution.

That Ádám had been appointed the highest level of professor without being coerced to convert to Christianity was proof of his gift for teaching and popularity as a teacher. With pervasive antisemitism, very few Jews were granted such recognition.

In 1901, Ádám was appointed Counsel to the Court of Emperor Franz Joseph. It was a title bestowed on those who had made significant career contributions and primarily given to ministers, high-level civil servants, industrialists, and academics. This too was a rare honor for Jews at that time.

Ádám Politzer and his students, circa 1875. Courtesy of Dr. Albert Mudry.

Ádám retired in 1907 at the age of 72. Five hundred physicians from around the world attended his retirement celebration. Today, over 100 years later, Ádám Politzer is still considered the father of otology and his name is recognized by ear-nose-and-throat doctors throughout the world. The author of 170 papers and four separate textbooks with several editions, he advanced the knowledge of otology, bringing about its recognition as an important medical specialty. He was an exceptional clinician, a tireless researcher, an innovator, and inventor. Above all he was a model professor, beloved by his students.

Family Man

The distance between Berlin and Vienna did not deter Ádám and Julie from having a close relationship with their three grandsons. Letters (many of which are in the Jewish Museum in Vienna) kept them connected between visits. Their conversations often centered around art. The boys had grown up surrounded by artists, singers, and musicians who visited their home. In spite of their youth, they were able to converse intelligently on matters of art.

Ádám's eldest grandson, Walter, was a talented artist. For Ádám's 70th birthday, Walter drew Dürer's "Madonna and Child," a gift that Ádám greatly treasured. Franz played the cello. Reinhold played the violin and enjoyed collecting art, which his grandfather encouraged with gifts to his collection.

Ádám's three grandsons: Walter, Reinhold, and Franz, circa 1900. Courtesy of Dr. Albert Mudry.

On August 3, 1906, ten months after Ádám's 70th birthday, Walter died. András found an article in the Budapest Journal that reported the details of that day. Apparently, Walter and a female friend, Adel Schreiber, went for a sunrise climb in the mountains. On their way down, Walter wanted to climb on a steep rock. Adel begged him not to do that. "Do not be a coward," scoffed Walter, right before he stumbled and fell to his death. Adel went to look for him, and also tripped, but was saved by a rock that stopped her fall.

Ádám was devastated by Walter's loss. But he found solace in the family that he had. He was close to many of his siblings, especially Zsigmond, Bernát, and Illés, and their children. He was listed as a witness at the weddings of two of Zsigmond's children: Margaret to László Léderer in November 1905 and Kornél Tőrők to Margaret Léderer in June 1915. He mentored Illés' son-in-law, Béla Bedő, (see **Chapter 9**) and may have mentored Margit Politzer, my great-grandmother, in art collecting.

Twelve years after Walter's death, tragedy struck once more. On October 20, 1918, Ádám's youngest grandson, Reinhold, died in an accident, according to Dr. Mudry. He was 20 years old. We were unable to locate records for further details.

Ádám and Julie with their grandchildren, Franz and Reinhold, circa 1908.
Courtesy of Dr. Albert Mudry.

World War I

Vienna was not a combat zone in World War I, but the war left its mark on the city's inhabitants. The euphoria and patriotic enthusiasm of the first months quickly waned as the war progressed. Massive shortages transformed daily life into an endless series of challenges for surviving with limited resources.

During the war, Ádám and Julie moved into a boarding house. Coal was so scarce that he could not heat their home. His friend, Sir St. Clair Thomson, a British surgeon and professor of laryngology, wrote in 1915 that "... every day, he (Ádám) walked from his boarding house to his beautiful apartment. In spite of his four-score years (80), he still occupied himself with art and research in otology. He was indeed a grand maître."

Last Will

Ádám was 75 years old when he wrote his first "Last Will" in 1910. He had considerable assets: a large home at 19 Gonzagagasse in the old quarter of Vienna where he lived in a spacious apartment and rented out other apartments, and a country home in a suburb of Vienna. He had valuable collections of artworks (see **Ádám Politzer: Artist, Art Collector, and Museum Founder on page 98**), medical and art history books, and anatomical models of the ear.

Given his assets, a will was an important document. He wanted to make sure his wife Julie, daughter Alice, and his grandsons were well taken care of. He derived great pleasure from the beauty of his collections. They were a symbol of a long and successful career. Ever the perfectionist, Ádám was meticulous about choosing who was to inherit each item. He wanted his heirlooms well taken care of and appreciated.

The executors of Ádám's will were chosen carefully from among his nephews: Gyula Politzer, my great-grandfather, Géza Politer, Illés' youngest son, and Dr. István Péterfi, his wife's nephew. These choices made sense. Gyula, a lawyer, was known among the family as being trustworthy, loyal, and kind-hearted, as told by Zsigmond in *Our Family History*. Géza, a businessman, was the favorite son of Ádám's favorite older brother, Illés. And István Péterfi was a successful lawyer. I recognized his name; he was a close friend of my grandfather, Sándor Ambrus (see **Chapter 13**).

In his will, Ádám gave generously to Jewish causes in Vienna and in his hometown of Alberti-Irsa, including funds donated to the Rabbi of Alberti-Irsa and the Rabbi of Abony, his grandfather Jakab Háy's hometown. He also left money for various organizations serving the poor, and in support of indigent medical students. His books on otology went to the University of Vienna library, his anatomical specimens to the Pathology Institute, and his illustrations of the ear to the Medical Society of Vienna.

Ádám wrote his first will after Walter's death. He bequeathed to Franz, his second grandson, the collection of letters from "my beloved, very talented grandson (Walter)." They were so important to Ádám that he stipulated to Franz that "not a single letter or any other relic be removed from this collection" and from time-to-time Franz should count them to verify this.

Like the improvements he made to his inventions and the refinements he made to his textbooks, Ádám amended his will twenty-two times over ten years. The last amendment, perhaps prompted by the death of Reinhold, was executed shortly before his passing.

On August 10, 1920, Ádám died at the age of 85. He was buried in the Jewish cemetery in Vienna. Sadly, his grave was destroyed during World War II.

The devaluation of the Austrian currency after World War I had a devastating impact on Ádám's widow, Julie. Destitute, like other widows before her, she was forced to put Ádám's extensive art collection on auction in 1922. Two catalogs were produced by the auctioneers Amsler and Ruthardt in Berlin and by I. Schwarz in Vienna. But no information could be found regarding the success of the auctions. Julie died eight years after Ádám, in 1928.

Ádám Politzer's Legacy

In his retirement speech in 1907, Ádám proclaimed, "No one can carry out in one short life all the projects that the need for activity produces. Man must consider himself happy if, by using his intellect and all the resources at his disposal, he can achieve at least a part of what he sets out to do." He had set out to do so much and accomplished more in his 85 years than most. Dr. Mudry wrote that he was "... an unusual and exemplary human being with immense qualities... He combined the skills of physician, researcher, teacher, historian, and artist."

Franz, Ádám's middle grandson, fought in World War I. Sometime after his return to Berlin, he changed his family name to Rőhn, a less Jewish sounding name, most likely due to the rise in antisemitism. His parents, Max and Alice, kept the Friedländer name. Living in Berlin was becoming increasingly difficult for Jews, even those who had converted, like the Friedländer family. Max died in 1934 at the age of 82. In July 1938, Franz and his widowed mother, Alice, emigrated to America. They were lucky to have escaped when they did; two months later Jews' passports were invalidated. Admittance into America was as challenging as escaping Germany, due to a nationwide reluctance to assist Jewish refugees. I presume that Alice used her father's and husband's extensive connections to emigrate.

Ádám and grandson Franz in his WWI uniform. Courtesy of Dr. Albert Mudry.

Settling in Los Angeles, Franz became an actor, photographer, and portrait painter. He died, single and childless in 1989, thus leaving Ádám with no living direct descendants.

In August 2019, my sister, two of my nieces and I visited Albertirsa and Ádám's childhood home, the synagogue where he had worshipped as a boy, and his statue in the town park. As I saw these places and his statue, he became real to me. I thought about his life, his incredible legacy. I felt proud to know him now. But wished that we, his family, had known more about him while we were growing up.

At Ádám Politzer's statue in Albertirsa, Hungary in 2022. Photo: Levente Tóth.

Dr. Politzer Ádám

1835 — 1920

A fülgyógyászat
úttöröje

LEARNING MORE

Ádám Politzer at the Centennial Exhibition of 1876 in Philadelphia

International Exhibitions in the 19th Century

The first world exhibition, "Great Exhibition of the Works of Industry of All Nations," took place in 1851 in a specially built "Crystal Palace" in London's Hyde Park. Over six million people traveled to London over six months to see technology and manufacturing wonders of the day. In her opening remarks, Queen Victoria heralded the exhibition as "the greatest triumph of peace which the world has ever seen." It began the golden age of world fairs, with more than forty international expositions held throughout the world, up until the start of World War I.

The international exhibitions of the 19th century were the contemporary equivalent of present-day social media. Enormous attendance figures far exceeded the reach of all other media. Leading industrialists, scientists, engineers, and academics from all over the world attended to learn the latest advancements in their field and to make new contacts. The exchange of ideas had a significant influence on and furthered scientific and technological innovation.

The Centennial Exhibition of 1876

The Centennial Exhibition, held in the US, was designed to celebrate the 100th anniversary of the Declaration of Independence. It was conceived to help restore national pride in the aftermath of the Civil War, Reconstruction, and economic depressions that occurred in the 1860s and

1870s. The political scene was rife with accusations of corruption and scandal within the Grant administration. The federal government approved the celebration but couldn't finance it due to the financial panic of 1873. Elite Philadelphians raised the necessary funds and planned the event.

It was the country's first World Fair. Philadelphia's Fairmont Park was lined with five large, topically designated pavilions and 250 smaller structures spread throughout 285 acres. Over 50,000 exhibits from 37 countries demonstrated the new industrial and technological advancements of the age, as well as the first international art exhibition.

Machinery Hall, the second largest building on the grounds, displayed massive American steam engines, intricate wood working machinery, and new inventions such as the telephone, the typewriter, and the mechanical calculator. It showcased America's industrial ingenuity. It helped to change the world's perception of the US from upstart to a world economic power.

Open from May through November 1876, the Centennial attracted 10 million visitors from around the world. It was a critical and financial success. Many exhibits became the nucleus for the Smithsonian Museum.

The Austrian Exhibit and the Politzer Collection

The Centennial propelled the field of otology and Ádám Politzer onto the world stage. The Austrian Exhibit occupied 24,070 square feet. Glass, pottery, furniture, clothing, and instruments were on display along with the Politzer Collection. The collection included 44 temporal bone dissections, 15 enlarged plaster models of the "membrana tympani" (eardrum), and an atlas of 24 watercolor sketches of various conditions of the membrana tympani, all created by Ádám Politzer. The extraordinary preparations of both normal and pathological specimens were "inspiring," as several otologists commented.

The exhibit was popular not only with physicians and scientists, but also with lay people. There was general interest in anatomy, many new discoveries were being described, and lectures in the field were being given to the general public. Furthermore, ear diseases were becoming more prevalent and yet were still poorly understood by the medical community.

Ádám's collection attracted attention in both the lay and medical presses. Most significantly, it received a judges' award, a considerable honor.

At the end of the Centennial, Ádám donated the collection to the Mutter Museum of the College of Physicians of Philadelphia. It became one of the museum's most distinguished exhibits.

Ádám's attendance and the presence of his collection at the Centennial had a profound impact on otology. Afterwards, the first International Congress of Otology was organized in New York. It was first in a series of international congresses that continued until World War I. The publicity relating to the Centennial and then later to the congresses attracted physicians from around the world to the field of otology. All wanted to be trained under Professor Politzer.

Artist, Art Collector, and Museum Founder

Ádám's artistic talent was evident at an early age. The work below was completed when Ádám was still in high school.

Ádám sketched the peasants on the Puszta (the Hungarian great plain) when he was in high school. Published in the *Medical Weekly* of Budapest, 1979.

In his art, as in his profession, the search for truth, perfection, and beauty inspired his work. As a physician, his artistic endeavors were primarily focused on illustrations of diseases of the ear, which he used for his clinical activities and teaching.

Ádám took every opportunity to indulge his passion for art. He was stimulated by visiting museums and art galleries. In his extensive travels, he acquired works of art for himself. He had many personal relationships with art connoisseurs and collectors at home and abroad. Some of his pieces were acquired at auctions, but more frequently, he bought pieces directly from artists. He particularly delighted in discovering new artists, as described in an article published in 1999 by Dennis Pappas, an otolaryngologist who researched Ádám's art collecting. Ádám fraternized with the great masters of his day, counting artists such as Charlemont, Probst, and Klimt as friends. They each created portraits of him that hung in his parlor.

Ádám loved to regale visitors to his home with stories about his art collection. And he had many visitors because in the afternoons after he saw patients in his clinic, he received and treated patients in his home.

Portrait of Ádám Politzer and his family by Hugo Charlemont, circa 1885.
Photo: Birgit and Peter Kainz, Vienna Museum.

I discovered a letter written on May 15, 1884, from one of Ádám's patients, Charles Edwin Wilbur (1833-1896), an American Journalist and Egyptologist. Wilbur had been deaf in one ear for over three years. On his trip to Egypt, he took a detour to Vienna to consult with Dr. Politzer. In the letter written to his wif, he described how he arrived at Ádám's home at 19 Gonzagagasse. The young servant who answered the door apologized that Ádám was running late but would soon return in his private coach. Wilbur was given a card numbered 22, so he had a long wait. Ushered into the parlor that doubled as a waiting room, he was amazed by the gallery of fine paintings; more than 76 paintings covered the walls. They kept him enthralled and helped him pass the time. After his medical examination, the conversation turned to the art collection, and he described how Ádám never tired of recounting the incidents and stories associated with their acquisition.

Portrait of Ádám by Ernst Klimt (Gustav Klimt's brother).

Courtesy of Josephinum – Ethics, Collections and History of Medicine, MedUni, Vienna.

Over 50 years, Ádám became a serious collector and recognized expert by art specialists and museum curators. His collection reflected his eclectic tastes. He cherished the old masters of the Renaissance, but also loved modern works by the up-and-coming artists of his time. He had an extensive collection of engravings, etchings, and, most notably, lithographs. Lithography, a process of printing from a stone or metal plate, was popular in France in the early 19th century. Ádám assembled a comprehensive collection that reflected the historical development of the art. He also had an excellent library on cultural objects and a collection of sculptures to complete his art collection.

In 1895, Ádám became one of the ten founding members of the Jewish Museum of Vienna. The purpose of the museum was the collection and preservation of Jewish history "from a literary, artistic, political, scientific, and historical point of view," according to Dr. Mudry's biography. Ádám donated over 132 items to the Jewish Museum of Vienna, a collection which the Nazis pillaged in World War II. Ádám served as the Chairman of the Board from 1912 until his death in 1920.

Ádám's portrait of his brother Illés, 1913. He painted two copies and gave each to Illés' daughters, Bertha and Reza. Courtesy of Semmelweis University Library.

FAMILY TREE

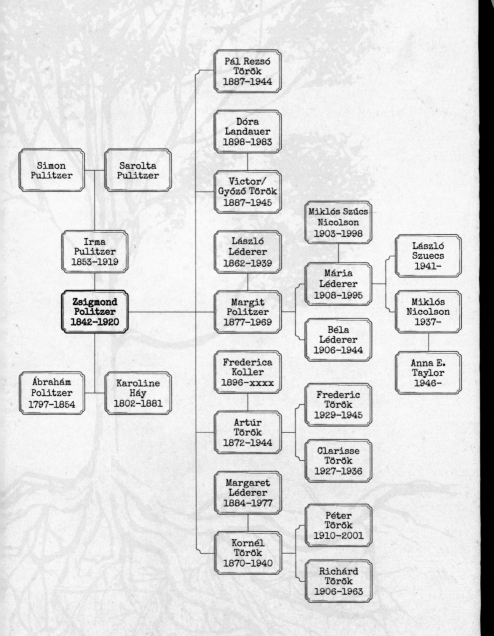

Simon Pulitzer

Sarolta Pulitzer

Irma Pulitzer
1853–1919

Zsigmond Politzer
1842–1920

Ábrahám Politzer
1797–1854

Karoline Háy
1802–1881

Pál Rezsó Török
1887–1944

Dóra Landauer
1898–1983

Victor/Gyózó Török
1887–1945

László Léderer
1862–1939

Margit Politzer
1877–1969

Frederica Koller
1896–xxxx

Artúr Török
1872–1944

Margaret Léderer
1884–1977

Kornél Török
1870–1940

Miklós Szúcs Nicolson
1903–1998

Mária Léderer
1908–1995

Béla Léderer
1906–1944

Frederic Török
1929–1945

Clarisse Török
1927–1936

Péter Török
1910–2001

Richárd Török
1906–1963

László Szuecs
1941–

Miklós Nicolson
1937–

Anna E. Taylor
1946–

Chapter 8

Zsigmond Politzer

Zsigmond (1842-1920) was the thirteenth of Ábrahám and Karoline's fourteen children. He was my great-great-great-uncle (five generations before me). Zsigmond grew up during the golden era of the Austro-Hungarian Empire. After a difficult childhood following the death of his father, Zsigmond became a visionary entrepreneur who contributed to Budapest's becoming a modern metropolis. But his exceptional accomplishments are not why I feel especially close to Zsigmond; his stories so vividly told in *My Family History* brought this family, my ancestors, to life for me. With his book as a starting point, I was able to learn so much more about them.

Grief

Zsigmond Politzer was devastated when he suddenly lost his father in 1854. Two months after Ábrahám's death, Zsigmond's mother, Karoline, sent him to secondary school in Pest. It was a different school than the Catholic school his older brothers had attended. Zsigmond's school was a non-religious sixth grade secondary science school, known as the Redoute, founded by the Austrian government after the revolution.

Starting halfway through the school year in the spring of 1855, Zsigmond, thirteen years old, found it difficult to catch up. Homesick and still mourning the premature death of his father (from appendicitis), he admitted to limited motivation: "I was a bad student, constantly daydreaming, and instead of doing homework and learning I spent my time reading and reading some more. I read books that were not adequate for my age but understood everything I read." He didn't like school and his professors didn't like him. In the third year he failed German literature and history, "since I was lazy." After consulting with his older siblings, he quit school.

He transferred to a private commercial school, the price of which was "outrageously high" and the quality low. The teachers were not well educated and poorly respected. As Zsigmond described it, "Most boarders left the school as smart as they had arrived." Although he was the best student, he didn't learn much, and left before the year was out.

"This was the beginning of a series of calamities. If I had stayed in school, I may not have become a doctor or lawyer, but at least I would have been well educated," Zsigmond wrote. In 1859, at age 17, he went to work for and live with his oldest brother Móricz, age 38, in a little courtyard apartment in Pest. Móricz had become a widower. His wife, Rosalie Klein, had died after six years of marriage, leaving him with the burden of raising three children. Móricz, a wool merchant, needed Zsigmond's help, but only on a seasonal basis.

Zsigmond didn't know his older siblings very well, mostly because of their age difference. "Móricz, Illés, Ignácz, Rudolf and Lena were all out of the house already by the time I was seven years old. They felt like strange guests when they would stop by." I understood how Zsigmond felt. Even in our family of seven siblings, it felt like we were two families: the older three, the younger three, and me in the middle. When my oldest sister married and moved out, my youngest brother was only five years old. They didn't get to know each other until much later.

With Zsigmond's father dead, his older brothers tried to help him find his path. But they had their own lives and interests. The siblings he was closest to, Ádám and Fanny, were not old enough to help.

In October, Zsigmond traveled 200 miles southeast of Budapest to the town of Dévaványa where his brother Fülöp leased a farm. Fülöp had also left school early to work in the farming business. Zsigmond's job was to collect wool every day from farmers in the area, which he carried home in a large backpack. He worked from sunup until sundown but felt little appreciated. "Fülöp treated me like a peddler, not so much as a kind word, with only meager rations of food."

By the end of the winter, badly nourished, physically and mentally weakened, Zsigmond regretted dropping out of school. He now had an all-consuming ambition to make something of himself, promising his mother to, "buckle down, to learn day and night, and to finish two grades in one year." Karoline, influenced by Fülöp's reports that Zsigmond was lazy and indolent, refused. "Mother did not want to invest any more money in me; I was a lost cause. I was stamped as lazy and no good."

Ambition and Focus

Zsigmond traveled 30 miles north to the town of Karcag, where Móricz had set up headquarters for the shearing season. He worked hard for Móricz, packing the collected wool, punching it down in big sacks, sewing the sacks shut, locking them up, and then organizing a wagon to be ready for a drop at five in the morning. That was just the start. Móricz's motto was: "Daytime is for work; nighttime is for calculating. Only animals need to eat, sleep, and rest."

Zsigmond described his round-the-clock labors:

> In an old farmer's wagon, pulled by two old horses and sitting on a wobbly seat way up high, we drove the whole night over bumpy roads to the next town where we spent the night at a peasant house. The courtyard was already full of farmers before sunrise wanting to sell their wool. We barely had enough time to wash up a bit, (when) another day of work began. We ate while we worked. Mostly we drank a glass of milk and ate a piece of bread. It was delicious. Towards the evening Móricz and I had our paperwork, accounting records, statistical logs as well as letter writing. Móricz was very fussy when it came to the accounting record. The register had to be right on. Not a penny less. Then it was night. Once again, I had to organize a wagon and following Móricz's other motto, 'the night is for traveling,' we drove to the next place to take charge of the goods there.

That is how Zsigmond spent his summer, with rest only on Sundays and holidays.

In September, Móricz sent Zsigmond and Fülöp east to buy wool and sign contracts for the next season. Zsigmond was likeable and smart – gifts that enabled him to make many good deals. "Good for Móricz. I did not earn anything. I was only promised to get a share later on. Yet I worked with devotion and commitment and did not rest."

It was hard work, but Zsigmond was happier with Móricz than with Fülöp. Móricz treated him like an equal, working alongside him. And he got a decent warm meal every day. Móricz was a good, honest, and fair man. Zsigmond remembers those days fondly. As he described in his memoir, "You learned a lot working for Móricz. It was a good life lesson: hard, but useful... It is amazing what a young man can endure. Humor played a big part, and this helped."

When the season was over, Zsigmond was sent to Abony, 50 miles west, to be with Rudolf. The brothers had decided for him; he had no choice in the matter. He felt like an indentured servant being passed to whomever needed him. After learning about commerce from their father, Rudolf had moved to Abony. He supplied the military with oats, straw, and hay. He also was the owner of the "regalian right," a license which allowed him to supply taverns with wine. Rudolf married Rozália Markbreit, and they had two sons and two daughters. Their oldest daughter, Jozefa, was my great-great-grandmother.

The winter working for Rudolf was tougher than working for Móricz and Fülöp and had lasting repercussions. Zsigmond's job was to collect oats from farmers. Measuring by weight was not common yet. Zsigmond had to manually count the scoops, as he transferred the oats into a receptacle. The ceilings of the attics were very low, so he was not able to stand straight during this back-breaking work. The attics lacked ventilation, with only a skylight for air. The scooping caused a thick dust, making it difficult to breathe. At times Zsigmond thought he was going to suffocate. At the end of a day, his spit looked like black ink.

"That winter planted the seed of illness in my lungs, which I suffered with all my life." In February 1860, Zsigmond became very ill with a bronchial infection. He returned to Pest, where his mother now lived. Together with brother Illés, by then a highly respected doctor, they nursed Zsigmond back to health. Seeing Zsigmond with such an illness, Illés got into a large argument with Rudolf, reprimanding him for being irresponsible with his little brother's welfare.

Zsigmond recovered and forgave Rudolf. Nevertheless, Zsigmond warned his readers, "If you have to work, make sure you do not work for a relative. The treatment and compensation are never in balance when you work for a relative. The relationship and respect are always at a much higher level when you work for a stranger."

In May 1860, Móricz sent Zsigmond to the Tisza region (the Northern Great Plain). Móricz assigned his brother to collect wool from four towns and the surrounding areas. Zsigmond was now experienced enough that Móricz trusted him to handle business on his own. Around that time, their sister Rosi, 21 years old, married Jakab Weiss. Jakab worked in his father's produce business in Debrecen. Although Zsigmond felt that his sister was too young to marry (she was three years older than Zsigmond), he didn't know at the time that his sister's marriage to Jakab would mark a turning point in his own life.

Success

Jakab Weiss and his father were about to sign a contract to supply the military in Nyíregyháza. This was 30 miles from Debrecen, too far for them to manage. They offered Zsigmond one-third of the business if he would move to Nyíregyháza and administer the contracts. Zsigmond, excited about the opportunity to work independently, asked Móricz for his approval. With Móricz's blessing came 2000 guilders, Zsigmond's share of the inheritance from his father. He used this to buy into the partnership and become a one-third business owner.

Zsigmond was eager to prove himself. He was excited to start a new life in which he supported himself and made his own decisions. After a few weeks of training in Debrecen, in September 1860, Zsigmond moved to Nyíregyháza. He rented a room on the edge of town near the marketplace. Across the street he rented a large granary to store oats and other produce, which he delivered to the military. A neighboring Jewish family cooked his meals, washed and mended his clothes, and supplied him with necessities when he went on business trips. He lived modestly, worked hard, and delivered quality products and excellent service for his customers. With one-third of the profits he was able to make ends meet.

Zsigmond was well liked by all the corporals. They felt at ease with him and trusted him. So much so, that during an emergency, they reached out to him first. In March 1861, a supply officer summoned Zsigmond in the middle of the night. There had been rumblings of uprisings due to waves of patriotism sweeping throughout Hungary. Emperor Franz Joseph had loosened his grip and reinstituted Hungarian as the official language and reinstated the Diet, Hungary's legislative body. Elections were held in

March and April. The Austrian regime needed to quell any potential rioting. Cavalry troops were arriving unexpectedly to several nearby towns the next day. They would need additional supplies beyond the contracted quantities right away.

With his newly acquired business sense, courage, and boldness, Zsigmond negotiated with the cavalry officer. He convinced the officer that prices would rise as soon as locals learned about the military's arrival, so it was in his best interest to accept Zsigmond's price increase. After they shook hands on the deal, Zsigmond left to purchase the required goods. Since he was able to pay above average for the goods, he quickly acquired all that he needed to fulfill the deal.

The following week his business partners, Jakab and his father, travelled to see Zsigmond. They were impressed with the way he had handled the negotiations, the fulfillment, and the resulting profits. Of course, it served them more than Zsigmond.

Zsigmond wrote, "My mother and brothers were quite impressed by the success I had. I finally proved myself to them. More importantly, though, I was..."

This is how Zsigmond concluded his story. He did not complete the sentence. This ending was testimony to his great humility. His son, who wrote the epilogue and published his book, wrote: "Without question, his last sentence, if finished, would have ended: 'More importantly, though, I finally was content with myself.'"

We know that Zsigmond stayed in Nyíregyháza for two years, but we don't know what happened with the business. Zsigmond described Jakab as "a reckless, careless man who burned through the assets and ended up deep in debt." Rosi and Jakab split up two years after their wedding. The marriage must have been deeply troubled. Divorce was rare at the time, especially for religious Jews. Jakab passed away shortly thereafter, "a scruffy, dissolute human being." Rosi, devastated and heartbroken from her awful marriage, moved to Pest to take care of their ailing mother. We must assume that Zsigmond followed her back to Pest.

The Jewish Emancipation Act

After the Austro-Hungarian Compromise of 1867, which partially re-established sovereignty of the Kingdom of Hungary, Budapest developed at an incredible speed, supported by the newly created Board of Public Works (1870). In 1868, the monarchy passed the Jewish Emancipation Act, which eliminated all barriers to Jewish participation in the economy and Budapest's development. Jews were bankers, financiers, merchants, lawyers, doctors, architects, journalists and estate managers and owners.

Zsigmond finished writing *Our Family History*, but there was so much more to tell. He briefly mentioned the third and fourth generation Politzers, his nephews and nieces. But he said little about his own family and nothing about his life after 1860. He had another 60 years ahead of him. He was not like Móricz, all work and no play. In his memoirs he stated that "...such a life under this regiment was sad and unalluring."

During the peace following the 1867 compromise and the fast pace of cultural and financial expansion, I could imagine Zsigmond – young, smart, ambitious, enterprising, personable – being at the center of activity.

Past and Present Meet

That may have been the end of this story had it not been for András in Hungary and Miklós Nicolson, Zsigmond's great-grandson who now lives in California. Among the many documents, letters, and photos in the box, I found an invitation to Miklós' wedding in 1965 in the US. On it was a handwritten note in Hungarian to Lili, my grandmother's sister who lived in Budapest. I mailed a letter to Miklós. His immediate reply started a wonderful series of communications. I was thrilled to find new family.

Miklós told me that his great grandmother was Irma Pulitzer, the cousin of newspaper magnate Joseph Pulitzer. Zsigmond married Irma Pulitzer sometime in the late 1860s. When I saw that name in the family tree book, I had assumed it was a misspelling. It wasn't. Irma was one of four daughters of Simon and Sarolta Pulitzer, Joseph Pulitzer's aunt and uncle.

Miklós and Anne Nicolson visiting our home in Virginia in 2019. From left to right: Steven Ambrus, Madeline Ambrus Lillie, Miklós, Anne, me and my husband Ed.

Vienna

We don't know how Irma and Zsigmond met or when they married. Their oldest son, Kornél (born Simon, he later changed his name to Kornél), was born in Budapest in 1870 when Zsigmond was 28 and Irma only 17. Calculating her age, I recalled Zsigmond's views on age and marriage; he had written that his sister Rosi was too young to marry at age 21. Yet he had married Irma when she was even younger. Had he fallen head over heels in love? Artúr was born two years later in Vienna. They stayed in Vienna where Margaret was born in 1877, as were the twins, Viktor (changed his name to Győző) and Pál Rezső, who arrived ten years later in 1887.

Vienna would have been alluring for Zsigmond and Irma. Zsigmond's favorite brother, Ádám, had established himself in Vienna by then. In the 1870s Ádám became the department head of the Otology (ear) Clinic of the Vienna General Hospital. Irma's three younger sisters moved to Vienna. The youngest sister, Szeréna (1867-1943), married a wealthy industrialist, August Léderer, and became a star of Viennese society at the turn of the century. She was renowned for her beauty as well as for being among the "best-dressed" in the city. Szeréna was among Klimt's most devoted patrons and the artist is said to have dined with her family every Friday evening.

With a lifelong passion for art (in his youth his father, Ábrahám, had recognized Zsigmond's talent and encouraged his painting), his thirst for adventure, and his devotion to family, Zsigmond, I imagine, must have reveled in his life during this time of religious and economic freedom and enjoyed the cultural gifts of Vienna and Budapest.

Zsigmond and Irma commuted between Vienna and Budapest (Buda merged with Pest in 1873). András found newspaper articles, wills, and many documents that mentioned Zsigmond Politzer. His task was difficult, not only because of the multiple spellings of Zsigmond's name (Siegmund, Sigmund, Zsigmund), but also because there were five Zsigmond Politzers living and working in Budapest at the same time.

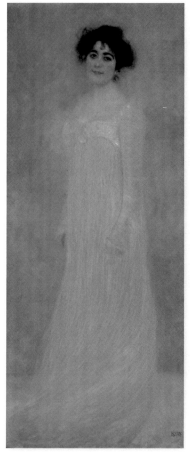

Painting by Gustav Klimt of Szeréna Pulitzer Léderer, Zsigmond's sister-in-law, 1899. Courtesy of the Metropolitan Museum of Art.

A Growing Empire

The newspaper articles told the story of a successful businessman. In 1872, in Pest, he ran a bank, Zsigmond Politzer & Company. Did this bank succumb in the 1873 stock market crash and the Great Depression (1873-1879) that followed? Or did he merge it with the Mercur publishing house? We don't know. We do know that from 1879, Zsigmond was the owner of the banking and bill exchange division of Mercur. In 1896, the Mercur bank, owned by Zsigmond and Kornél, became a shareholding company.

The bill of exchange department of Mercur operated a gambling business which issued Kincsem lottery tickets. For a single forint, ticket holders had a chance to win the jackpot of 50,000 forints (the equivalent of $725,000 in today's dollars). The lottery was named after Kincsem (1874-1887), a thoroughbred racehorse that still holds the record for the most wins of any unbeaten racehorse. My father had often told us stories about this magnificent horse. Kincsem was to Hungarians what Seabiscuit was to Americans, an underdog providing hope and pride during a depression.

Advertisement for a Kincsem lottery ticket in the *Pesti Hirlap*, 1885.

In *Our Family History*, Zsigmond warned his readers not to work for a relative. Yet he did not heed his own advice. His nephew, Alexander Politzer (Illés' son) was the business manager for the gambling business. His own son, Kornél, was a co-founder of the Mercur bank. The bank may have acted somewhat like a merchant/investment bank, with investments in the Hungarian Transport Company (railways were exploding) and the Hungarian Automobile Company.

Zsigmond invested in real estate. He owned land as well as office and apartment buildings throughout Budapest. Between 1897 and 1903, the Elizabeth Bridge, a beautiful suspension bridge named after Empress Elizabeth, wife of Emperor Franz Joseph, was built connecting Buda and Pest. A piece of land was freed up in what was then called Eskü square. Zsigmond and his partners purchased the land and built the impressive headquarters of the Mercur Banking and Bill of Exchange on this lot between 1900-1901.

The address later became Váci utca No. 37. (Budapest's 5th Avenue). Zsigmond's son, Kornél Török; daughter, Margaret Politzer Léderer and her husband; and Gyula Kelemen, a director of Mercur, all lived on the first floor of the building (it would be the second floor in an American building). József Rippl-Rónai, the famous Hungarian painter, lived on the second floor between 1902 and 1904 and had his studio in the attic.

Margaret described to Miklós, her grandson, how their apartment was a museum of artwork. Guests at their parties included intellectuals, writers, artists, scientists, and politicians. Young men who became famous scientists in America, such as Edward Teller, were friends of her children, Béla and Maria.

The Mercur Bank, designed by Artúr Meinig, was built in 1901 at what is now Váci utca No. 37. Photo circa 1904. The building was demolished in 1960-1961. Metropolitan Ervin Szabó Library, Budapest / Budapest Collection

Zsigmond built a large apartment building on Teréz körút, across the street from his niece, Jozefa Politzer Misner, my great-great-grandmother. Three of Zsigmond's children lived with their families at Teréz körút 47 until their deaths in 1944/1945 (World War II).

Teréz körút 47 was built by
Zsigmond Politzer in 1888.
Fortepan / Budapest Főváros
Levéltára / Városrendezési és
Építészeti Osztályának fényképei.

The facts gleaned from newspaper stories and documents are impressive. Zsigmond served on the "Supervisory Committees" of the Transylvanian Hungarian Mortgage and Credit Bank and the Hungarian Railway Company. He was President of the Bankers and Exchange Brokers Association. In 1897, he attended a conference on the reform of the Stock Exchange where he delivered a speech pushing for transparency of trading on the Stock Exchange.

Zsigmond's warning of the need for transparency and protection from greedy and corrupt practices would be as relevant today as it was then. His speech was a courageous act. To stand up to power is no small thing. It reminded me of my parents' story (see **Chapter 15**).

The newspaper stories also reported on their glamorous social lives. András found an article in the Fővárosi Lapok (Gazette of the Capital), dated Sunday January 22, 1884, describing a costume ball hosted by widow Lady Sarolta Pulitzer. The guests arrived at nine o'clock in the evening and left at seven the following morning after the third "fiery" czarda, the traditional Hungarian dance that begins slowly and ends with couples whirling around the dance floor at an exhilarating fast pace.

I pictured the formal ball from *The Sound of Music* and imagined Zsigmond and Irma's charmed life at the height of his career. Zsigmond benefited from and contributed to the golden age of Budapest and its growth as a modern metropolis.

This boy, whose mother and brothers had once called lazy, became a hardworking, prosperous entrepreneur. I wish I had known this story when I pursued a business career against my parents' wishes. What a welcome dose of bravery and confidence it would have provided.

When Zsigmond, 78 years old, died on October 15, 1920, twenty months after the death of Irma, he left behind five children and four grandchildren. His favorite brother, Ádám, had died two months earlier in August. Of his thirteen siblings, only Rosa, Fülöp and Gusztáv survived him. As Zsigmond had mourned his own father, Ábrahám, and wrote about him with the utmost love and admiration, so Kornél wrote about Zsigmond. "We, his children, and those who follow, his grandchildren and great-grandchildren shall never forget him and remember him with love and pride. Let's hope that we are all worthy of him in life and work."

Jewish Assimilation

Kornél, as Zsigmond described, had "a sense of family and a warm heart." He married Margaret Léderer. Their two children grew up in Belgium, where Kornél became Chief Consul at the Embassy of the Hungarian Kingdom (1922-1940). After World War I, with the Hungarian economy and society in distress, Kornél was instrumental in bringing 13,000 Hungarian children to Brussels as part of the Belgian-Hungarian Child Relief Project. In 1940, when the Germans invaded Belgium, a bomb exploded next to Kornél, ending his life.

Zsigmond's four sons, including Kornél, changed their surname to Török in 1898. Seemingly at odds with their devotion to their father and his family, it was consistent with the strong Hungarian national sentiments of the times and compatible with growing Jewish assimilation into Hungarian culture. At that time, Hungary included the present-day states of Slovakia and Croatia, and parts of Serbia, Romania, and Ukraine. Hungary encouraged Jews to change their names to Hungarian surnames in an effort to tip the demographic balance between nationalities within the Austro-Hungarian empire. With Jews considered Hungarians and speaking the Hungarian language, Hungarians would attain a majority. Politzer was a German-sounding Jewish name. Török was a popular Hungarian name, meaning Turkish.

Kornél Török, Zsigmond's oldest son, in his official uniform as Chief Counsel to Belgium, circa 1922. Courtesy Nicolson Family.

Margaret Politzer Léderer, Zsigmond's daughter and Miklós' grandmother. Courtesy Nicolson Family.

László Léderer (Margaret's husband) with grandson, Miklós, circa 1938. Courtesy Nicolson Family.

In addition to changing their names, all four sons converted to Christianity. It is not obvious why they converted or when. Their sister Margaret did not convert. (see **Margaret Was Not Allowed to Pursue Her Dreams on page 118**).

How religious were Zsigmond and Irma? At first I thought not, as Zsigmond did not own prayer seats in the Dohány Synagogue like many of his brothers. Later, I learned that he chose to own seats at the Rumbach Synagogue, which was more conservative at the time. The Jewish religion was an important part of Zsigmond and Irma's identity. In the codicil to their wills (we could not find the original wills), they stipulated payments to the Jewish boys' orphanage, the Chief Rabbi of Irsa, the Jewish community of Irsa, and the Jewish community of Makó (where Irma grew up). They also left money to the Chevra Kadisha of Irsa, "with the purpose of remembering me and my wife during the services of the Jewish high holidays…. and to light the usual candle on the day of our deaths, and at the same time, say Kaddish for me and my wife."

I wondered if Zsigmond and Irma did this because they knew that their sons, who had converted, could not. But having Kaddish said for them, was so important they paid the synagogue to ensure that it would.

Zsigmond Politzer Family Tombstone: Crypt No 34 (L) at the Kozma Street Cemetery, Budapest, Hungary. Photo: Levente Tóth

LEARNING MORE

Margaret Was Not Allowed to Pursue Her Dreams

Miklós, my newly found cousin in California, told me about his grandmother Margaret. She was a talented pianist and loved to play. Her teachers included the famous musician Béla Bartók. Margaret's mother, Irma, would only let her play for family and friends. Adhering to the social norms of the day, Irma felt that a career as a pianist was not suitable for a young lady of her "breeding."

One day Margaret happened to be playing at a resort where they were vacationing. Eugene d'Albert, the great pianist of his time, heard her play and asked her to become his student, an unusual request from this maestro. Typically, it was the other way around; promising pianists begged him to become their teacher. But even he could not persuade Irma.

Margaret married László Léderer (no relation to her uncle). László Léderer's ancestors were wealthy landowners from the southern Transdanubia region of Hungary. László founded the Association of Jewish School Teachers and was a large donor to sick Jewish teachers.

Margaret became blind in her 60s, at a time which coincided with the rise of the Nazis and the Holocaust. She abandoned her music. She donated her Bechstein piano (Europe's equivalent to the Steinway) to the Budapest Music Academy. But after she escaped to the US (during the 1956 Revolution), her son, Miklós' father, bought her a piano. Joyfully, she played again until she died.

Báboczka.

The Léderer estate at Báboczka, Hungary. It was destroyed by the Russians after World War II. Courtesy Nicolson Family.

FAMILY TREE

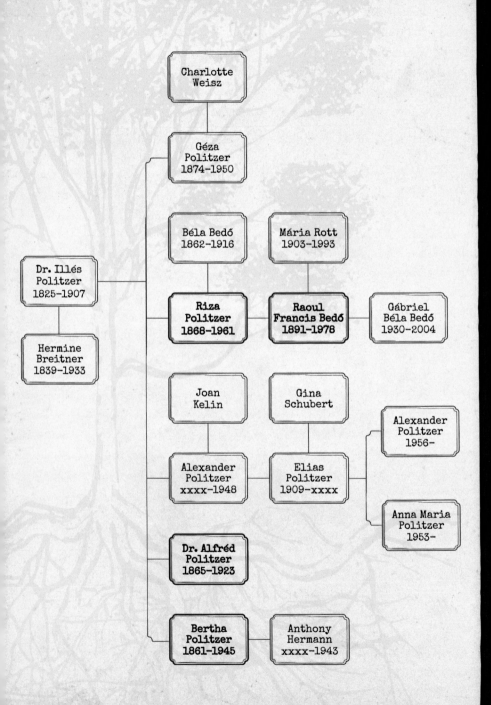

Chapter 9

Illés Politzer's Children

Two of Illés' five children, Alfréd (1865-1923) and Riza (1868-1961), especially piqued my interest because they were close friends of my great-grandmother Margit. Like Margit, they shared a love of art and art collecting. To learn about their life is also a way to learn about Margit, a way to travel back in time and connect to both Margit and to my grandmother Bözsi. Riza's son, Rudi, an illustrious art collector, advised Margit in art collecting. His wife, Maria, continued to be close to my grandmother Bözsi until her death in 1985.

To learn about Bertha, a writer and Illés' oldest daughter, was a revelation. Bertha's stories were published, an amazing accomplishment for women writers, and even more so for Jewish women writers, at the turn of the 20th-century. Her story is told in the sidebar.

Illés' other two sons, Alexander and Géza, were successful businessmen. I know little about them and therefore did not include them in this chapter.

Alfréd a Notable Art Collector

Alfréd, the second oldest of Illés' children, became the chief physician at the Budapest Children's Hospital. In spite of his elevated position, he took care of his nieces and nephews. I found a note from my grandmother, Bözsi, in which she wrote that she and her sister, Lili, disliked Alfréd because he prescribed cod liver oil when they were young girls.

Alfréd served as a reserve soldier in the military and was awarded the Knight's Cross of Franz Joseph, though we don't know for what reason.

Much to his parents' disappointment, Alfréd never married. He was devoted to collecting art. He was friends with Marcell Nemes (1866-1930), one of the most significant art collectors in early 20th-century Hungary. When Alfréd took his young nephew, Rudi Bedő (see below), to visit Nemes' home, he was most proud that Rudi could identify the painters of Nemes' collection: El Greco, Picasso, Cézanne, Degas, Manet, Monet, and Renoir, among others. At Nemes' soirées, Alfréd would have socialized with contemporary artists, such as the well-known Hungarian painter Jozsef Rippl-Rónai (1861-1927), as well as art critics and museum experts.

In 1914, the magazine *Ország Világ* published a short article about Alfréd and his art collection. They described his collection as "grandiose" and worthy of an international reputation. Alfréd enjoyed 17th-century Italian masters as well as contemporary Hungarian and German artists. But his passion was collecting pictures of Emperor Franz Joseph and his wife, Sisi.

Alfréd died in 1923. He was 58 years old.

Alfréd Politzer, circa 1910.

Alfréd photographed in his drawing room among his paintings for an article in the magazine *Ország Világ*, 1914.

A Family's Love of Art

Riza, Illés and Hermine's fourth child, was born in 1868. At age 22, she married Béla Bedő and a year later, in 1891, gave birth to her one and only child, Raoul Francis Bedő, nicknamed Rudi.

An entrepreneur, Béla built a highly successful chemical company, which mined gold and manganese and produced sulfuric acid and gunpowder. Riza and Béla enjoyed traveling and, rather than leave their young son at home with the nanny, they took him along. Their favorite activity was frequenting museums and art galleries in Italy, Vienna, and throughout their travels. Rudi learned to love art and developed a lifelong passion for it. His Christmas wishes were always for art history books.

The celebration of Christmas among Jewish families was a topic of great debate, particularly among Neolog (reform) Jews. *Equality, (Egyenlőség)*, the most influential Jewish weekly of the time, wrote with outrage and indignation about the widespread prevalence of Christmas trees and gifts among Jewish citizens. On the other hand, the *Sabbath Newspaper* wrote in 1882, "Christmas is a celebration of children and parents are happy to bring joy to their children." Many Hungarians saw Christmas as a secularized holiday and assimilated Jewish families found their own balance between celebrating Christmas and Chanukah.

In 1903, Béla commissioned Emil Vidor, an outstanding architect of the era, to build a home on Honvéd utca, a twelve-minute walk from Riza's parents' home. It was a second home for them, as Béla's business was based in Nagyvárad (today Oradea, Romania), approximately 200 miles east of Budapest.

Together with my older sister and two nieces, I visited Budapest in 2019. I wanted to meet with András and see the places that were important to our family. András arranged a special tour of the Bedő house, including one of the upstairs private apartments. "Stunning, unique, exquisite." Those were our reactions to the ornamentation, metal work, lead glass, and dramatic ceramic tiled staircase. Most astonishing: house, owners, and contents had survived World War II. Today, it stands as one of the finest examples of Art Nouveau architecture in Budapest.

From left to right: Ignácz Misner, Riza Politzer Bedő, unidentified woman, and Béla Bedő, circa 1895.

Bedő House, Honvéd utca, Budapest. Photo 2019.

Rudi Bedő: Art Collector and Patron of the Arts

My father told me about Rudi, Riza and Béla's son, though he never mentioned his name. I knew him as the relative who lost a leg in World War I and was an art expert. My great-grandmother Margit, who loved to collect art, would often ask Rudi to advise her on her purchases. My father remembered Rudi, "When my uncle came to critique a painting or a piece of furniture, he would first ask Margit if she had already purchased it. If she said yes, he would tell her what a fine purchase she had made. If she answered that she was considering it, he would give her an honest critique".

Rudi wrote an autobiography in the 1960s, which András was never able to locate. It was referenced in an article written by Péter Molnos for the Kieselbach Gallery in 2010, *Passion and Knowledge: The Bedő Collection and Its Place In History*. Molnos wrote that the Bedő Collection "stands as a monument to Rudolf Bedő's achievement, personality, and collection, demonstrating the sophisticated taste, great knowledge, and passion of the collector."

The article described how Rudi, inspired by his uncle Alfréd and his great uncle, Ádám Politzer, became passionate about art. At age 12, he bought a Hungarian lithograph, the first acquisition for what would become his impressive art collection. His acquisitions would be put on hold due to World War I.

Rudolf Bedő, cavalryman in World War I.

At the outbreak of World War I, Rudi joined the military as a 1st lieutenant. In September 1914, the Russian army grossly outnumbered the Austro-Hungarian forces in the eight-day Battle of Rava Ruska (Ukraine). Austro-Hungarian forces suffered major losses. Captured by Russians, Rudi was taken to a hospital in Kiev (Kyiv, Ukraine) where they amputated his left leg. In 1915, Rudy returned to Hungary in a prisoner exchange and was decorated for his courage and valiant efforts.

Shortly after his return, his father died. At age 25, Rudi became head of his family and his father's company. Now, he could indulge his artistic passion and become a serious collector.

His home, near the chemical company, was close to Nagybánya, a center for art. The Nagybánya artist colony was founded as a summer retreat for artists in the 1890s. It grew into a preeminent artists' school and was a significant influence in the development of 20th-century Hungarian and Romanian art.

Rudi developed close relationships with many of the artists, often supporting them financially. Rudi also enjoyed photography, as described in Molnos' article:

> ...a beautiful series of photos of the town and the surroundings... are proof of Bedő's outstanding artistic standards and excellent technical skills...and show the collector's attraction to the town and his insatiable passion for collecting."

In Budapest, Rudi continued to maintain a close relationship with Marcell Nemes, the prominent collector his uncle Alfréd had introduced him to as a young boy. Molnos' article described their relationship:

> Though the Nemes collection contained more valuable items, the basic characteristics and typical features of the two collections are quite similar. They both had an absolutely wide field of interest, and both were enthusiastic about old carpets, antique furniture, Gothic and Baroque painting and contemporary Hungarian art. Their absolute Hungarian favorite was József Rippl-Rónai. Both collections contained many paintings by Rippl-Rónai, whereas Nemes owned the most valuable pieces of the oeuvre.

Rudi constantly changed and expanded upon the collection in their house on Honvéd utca, Budapest. Molnos' article described how:

> Bedő had a strong aesthetic sense with which he was able to arrange the antique furniture, paintings, sculptures, and ornaments in his private museum in an artistic way.

I had toured the house. It was easy to imagine how magnificent it must have been before the war.

In the late 1920s, Rudi married Maria Rott. In 1930, they had a son, Gabriel Béla Bedő, nicknamed Gabi. With antisemitism on the rise, they baptised their son and the family converted to Christianity. This was not unusual for Hungarian Jews at the time. Several Politzer family members also converted: Ádám's daughter, Alice Friedländer, and her family, and Zsigmond's four sons: Kornél Török, Artúr Török, Győző Török and Pál Rezső Török.

Maria Rott Bedő and Rudi Bedő in 1931.

In 1939, when the Germans invaded Poland, Rudi was given permission by the director of the Hungarian Museum of Fine Arts to send a large portion of his collection to England. He sent 76 items, including paintings, drawings, sculptures, and industrial art craft pieces. After England's declaration of war in 1941, the collection was seized by the English army and auctioned off. The remainder of his collection, housed at his home (the Bedő House), shockingly survived the war.

By 1942, their conversion to Christianity offered no protection. Nor did Rudi's decorations for his courage in World War I. Starting in 1938, a series of anti-Jewish laws, called Numerus Clauses, restricted Jewish education, occupation, and civil rights. Jews were no longer allowed to own and run businesses. Rudi's company was taken over by the government. When the Nazis took over Hungary in October 1944, the family was issued a letter of protection from the Swiss Consulate in Budapest. Remarkably, the family and their home survived the war intact.

Several years after the war, in a letter to a friend, Rudi wrote,

> *Art collecting is a very nice thing. I did it too, as long as I could, until 1944. Nowadays, I am rather interested in selling, or, so to say, I would be interested in selling, because here it is not possible to sell a work of art, it is only possible to fritter it away.*

He survived by writing articles, books and reviews of art magazines and selling off the remainder of his collection. Rudi made sure that many of his pieces went to Hungarian institutions: the Museum of Fine Arts, Museum of Applied Arts, the Hungarian National Gallery, and the Hungarian Jewish Museum.

LEARNING MORE

Bertha Politzer Herrmann: A Writer Ahead of Her Time

Bertha (1861-1945), Illés and Hermine's oldest daughter, married Antal, a merchant who struggled financially. They had no children. With considerable support from Illés, they were able to live out their lives comfortably.

Bertha became a writer. Between 1899 and 1901, four of her short stories were published in the *Almanac of Israelite Hungarian Literary Society*. This was a remarkable feat for a woman of that time. Margit Kaffka, generally regarded as Hungary's first major woman writer, did not publish until ten years later.

András found two of Bertha's four published works. I wondered if her fictional portrait of a Jewish family may have been autobiographical. The "fictional" wife loved Russian literature – Turgenev and Dostoevsky. The husband's pawn shop struggled financially, but when he became a stockbroker, their financial wealth grew.

András described how Bertha's writing was authentic and remarkable in its style, using contemporary idioms of the working class. Her empathy and compassion for the everyday person was evident.

Bertha was only 39 years old when her last story was published. We don't know what happened to her writing career after that. Nor do we know much else about her. She was 84 when she died on January 25, 1945, during the war. She may have died of natural causes. Or by bullets of the Arrow Cross on the banks of the Danube. Or on a forced march. We will never know.

FAMILY TREE

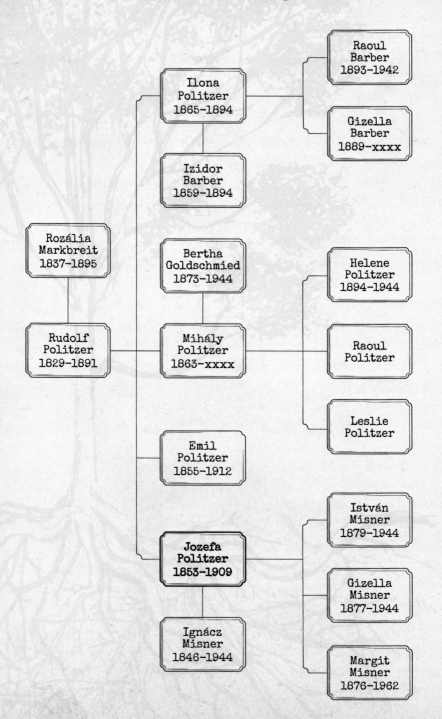

Raoul
Barber
1893-1942

Gizella
Barber
1889-xxxx

Ilona
Politzer
1865-1894

Izidor
Barber
1859-1894

Rozália
Markbreit
1837-1895

Bertha
Goldschmied
1873-1944

Helene
Politzer
1894-1944

Rudolf
Politzer
1829-1891

Mihály
Politzer
1863-xxxx

Raoul
Politzer

Leslie
Politzer

Emil
Politzer
1855-1912

István
Misner
1879-1944

Jozefa
Politzer
1853-1909

Gizella
Misner
1877-1944

Ignácz
Misner
1846-1944

Margit
Misner
1876-1962

Chapter 10

Jozefa Politzer Misner

Jozefa Politzer Misner (1853-1909) was Zsigmond's niece, born to Rudolf Politzer (the fifth of Ábrahám and Karoline's fourteen children). Jozefa was my great-great-grandmother, four generations before me. There is little information about her. From what little I know, even after her death, she was a beacon of light that gave my great-great-grandfather, Ignácz Misner, strength in his darkest hours.

Pure Joy

I first learned about Jozefa in *Our Family History*. Zsigmond recounted that Jozefa, his niece, dazzled his parents, Ábrahám and Karoline, from the moment they saw her. "Ábrahám said that he has never seen a more beautiful child, inside and out, who was able to spread such joy around her by just entering a room. He predicted that she would be someone special."

In the 19th century, women's stories rarely made the papers. Except for birth and death certificates, official documents were the provenance of men. Adolf Ágai (1836-1914), a Hungarian Jewish journalist who wrote about Hungarian Jewish life, observed, "... only men have histories. Famous women are as rare as bald women...As a matter of fact, respectable women do not have a history. They are born, marry, help their husbands, raise children and die." Clearly, he was a man of his time. I could not imagine one making such statements today.

To tell Jozefa's story, I puzzled together whatever bits and pieces I could find: Zsigmond's brief description in *Our Family History*, a reference in my uncle Gábor Virány's book and family tree, an inscription on a gravestone, a donor plaque (see **Donor Plaques on page 140**).

Young Jozefa

Jozefa's mother's family, the Markbreits, were long-standing residents of Abony, where her father's grandfather, Jakab Háy lived. The Politzer/ Háy and Markbreit families were such close friends that the Politzer children referred to Jozefa's grandmother as "Aunt Esther." According to Zsigmond, Rozália Markbreit, Jozefa's mother, was beautiful. Rozália and Rudolf (the 5th Politzer sibling) married shortly after Rudolf moved to Abony to start his own business – supplying the military with oats, hay and straw, and the taverns with wine (see **Chapter 8**).

When they married, Rudolf was twenty-three and Rozália fifteen. I confirmed the dates with András to ensure the accuracy of the translation. Rozália's death notice in 1895 stated, "at the age of 58, after many years of suffering, endured with faith in God and unparalleled calm..." There was no mistake. She was fifteen when she married Rudolf and sixteen when she gave birth to Jozefa. It was unusual for women to be married that young; Rudolf's sisters were all much older. I was suspicious the marriage was necessitated by Rozália's pregnancy.

Jozefa was born on January 22, 1853. Shortly after, Rozália went to Karlsbad (Karlovy Vary in Bohemia or today the Czech Republic) to "recover from an ailment." The town was the site of numerous hot springs and developed a famous spa resort for the European aristocracy in the 19th century. While Rozália recuperated in Karlsbad, Rudolf brought Jozefa to Alberti to be cared for by Karoline and Ábrahám.

What kind of illness did she suffer from? We don't know. I wondered what kind of mother Rozália was, being a child herself. What kind of mother left her infant? I imagined a selfish scenario: Rozália went with her mother to pamper herself at the spa while relinquishing care of her child to her in-laws. But it was also possible that she did have an ailment. Her obituary described many years of suffering. I had read numerous obituaries of women relatives that had used the same words, describing death after "many years of suffering." We will never know the truth.

Jozefa was Ábrahám and Karoline's third grandchild, one of 56 next generation Politzers, and their favorite. Zsigmond described how Ábrahám and Karoline were struck by Jozefa from the moment they saw her, when they commented on her spreading joy just by entering a room. Unfortunately, Ábrahám did not get to see his granddaughter Jozefa grow up; he died the following year.

Zsigmond, equally enamored, wrote, "She (Jozefa) was always happy and smiling... She was the adornment of the family." Zsigmond, eleven years old when Jozefa was born, must have felt more like an older brother than an uncle.

Jozefa was almost six years old when Zsigmond came to work for his older brother, Rudolf, in that "fateful winter of 1859/1860." I wondered what kind of father Rudolf would have been given his callous treatment of Zsigmond (described in **Chapter 8**.) Did he learn to be more caring, after his older brother Illés reprimanded him?

Rudolf's business prospered and he and Rozália lived comfortably with Jozefa and her siblings: Emil, Mihály, and Ilona. He bought a permanent seat in the Dohány Synagogue in Budapest, an expensive, curious investment given his residence in Abony, suggesting that his Jewish faith must have been important to him.

Jozefa's childhood home in Abony, Hungary.

The remaining shell of the synagogue in Abony, Hungary. Photo 2019.

Jozefa with her father, Rudolf Politzer, circa 1863.

Jozefa Builds a Family

On August 17, 1875, Jozefa married the "very distinguished" Ignácz Misner (see **Chapter 11**). She was 22 years old and Ignácz was 29. Did they meet in Abony or in Budapest? Did her uncle Zsigmond introduce them? With his banking business and real estate holdings, Zsigmond may have befriended the up-and-coming lawyer and played matchmaker.

I imagined Jozefa traveling to Budapest with her father to visit her grandmother, Karoline, who had moved to Budapest after Ábrahám's death, or to worship at the Dohány Synagogue for the Jewish high holidays.

Ignácz and Jozefa moved to 5 Gizella Square in Budapest, not far from Illés and Hermine's home. A year after being married, Jozefa gave birth to Margit, my great-grandmother. Gizella was born the following year and István (Hungarian for Steven) was born in 1879. Zsigmond wrote, "Just like Jozefa, her children were happy and always smiling ... All were carbon copies of their perfect parents." Their stories are shared in Chapters 11 and 12.

Jozefa raised her children during the golden age of Budapest. It was a time of extended peace and economic growth. As Jews, the next generations were not only accepted but welcomed by the political and business elite. Jews played leading roles in the many technological, scientific, and medical advancements of the time. Although their lives were woven into every fabric of Hungarian culture, Jews were rarely accepted into social clubs, sporting clubs, and elite social circles. They were not protected from antisemitism and seeds of intolerance appeared in newspaper articles, political debates, university classrooms and even religious sermons.

In 1894, Hungarian and German physicians began a crusade against tuberculosis. (see **Tuberculosis: The 19th Century White Plague on page 141**). But it was too late for Jozefa's sister, Ilona. In March of that year, at the age of 29, Ilona died of the disease. Her husband, Izidor Barber, a wool merchant, died four months later, also of tuberculosis. They left behind two young children, Gizella and Raoul. Jozefa must have been terribly distressed to learn that Izador's father was granted guardianship. Jozefa and Ignácz were to play only a back-up role.

Jozefa and Ignácz Misner, circa 1908.

When I examined the few pictures I have of Jozefa, I saw a stoic, elegant woman. Maybe it was the way she set her jaw, that said she had experienced the good and bad life had to offer. I imagined she was determined to protect her family and give them the best life she could.

Life Stories from Gravestones

Jozefa was 38 years old when her father, Rudolf, died in 1891 at the age of 62. Her mother died four years later (1895) at the age of 58.

When I visited Budapest in 2019, András, Kati Bardi (a translator and friend) and I drove to Abony to search for family graves. The Jewish graveyard was indistinguishable from the backyard forest behind the caretaker's home. There hadn't been much caretaking. Many of the gravestones had been knocked to the ground and those standing were overgrown with vines that we pulled away to read the inscriptions. We found many graves of the Háy family, though not Jozefa's great-grandfather Jakab Háy.

Rudolf and Rozália's gravestones in Abony, Hungary. Photo: Levente Tóth 2022.

Jozefa Politzer Misner, circa 1900.

We found several Markbreits, Jozefa's mother's family. And we found Rudolf and Rozália, side by side.

Their gravestones were almost five feet tall. Etched on one side of the dark granite stones were inscriptions written in Hebrew. András had them translated.

> *Here rests Rudolf Politzer, the unforgettable husband and best father*
> *... He is mourned by his sad widow, loving children, and relatives.*
> *May his memory be blessed forever.*

> *Here rests the unforgettable and gentlest mother (Rozália) ...*
> *She is mourned by her sad children and grandchildren. May her*
> *memory be blessed forever.*

I immediately regretted my imagined harsh assessments of Rudolf and Rozália as parents. I will never know the truth. But I gave them the benefit of the doubt, and pictured them as doting, wonderful parents.

We found the gravestone of Emil, Jozefa's younger brother, who died in 1912, at the age of 57, three years after Jozefa. I presumed that Jozefa and Emil had been close because Emil lived in one of the apartments in the large home built by Jozefa and Ignácz, where they also lived. (see **Chapter 11**). There were two to four apartments on each of three floors. The apartments were not rented out but given to family members. I wondered if Jozefa and Emil had a close relationship to their younger brother, Mihály. Family, I believe, was important to them, both in life and in death. Mihály brought Emil's body from Budapest back to Abony for burial.

We could not find Mihály's gravestone nor those of his family. His marriage to Berta Goldschmied produced two sons and a daughter. Both sons were decorated veterans of World War I while Berta worked in the Red Cross Hospital. In 1921, Mihály, retired as a railway engineer, was head of the Jewish school board in Abony. We don't know when he or his two sons died. Berta, 71 years old, and their daughter Ilona, 50 years old, were killed in Auschwitz in 1944.

138

Eternal Love

Jozefa died of a heart attack on February 10, 1909, at the age of 56. She died in a private hospital, the Herczel sanatorium for surgical, internal medicine, and women patients. Her obituary in the newspaper, *Pesti Hírlap*, said she passed away after prolonged suffering. Did she suffer from a weakened heart, the result of exposure to tuberculosis from her sister Ilona? We will never know. On her tomb in the Jewish cemetery on Kozma Street, Budapest, is inscribed in Hebrew under her name and the date of her death, "She died in good name on Shevat 19th, in 5669."

Ignácz never remarried. He remained in love with Jozefa for the rest of his life. Every year, he visited her grave on the anniversary of their wedding and on the anniversary of her death, until 1944 when the Holocaust and Ignácz's health made a visit impossible. In June 1944, he was forced to leave his home and his belongings. Gábor Virány, my father's cousin, wrote in his book, titled *Az újabbik Balogh (The Tailor Balogh)*, that his heart broke when he could not take the painting of his beloved Jozefa.

Painting of Jozefa that Ignácz was forced to leave behind. Photo found in box in my parents' home.

LEARNING MORE

Donor Plaques

On our 2019 Budapest trip, we visited the Jewish cemetery on Kozma Street. Inside the mortuary, plaques from several destroyed institutions throughout Budapest were displayed. I found the names of Ignácz and Jozefa Misner inscribed on several large marble plaques, including two from a hospital where they had donated hospital rooms. They were generous donors throughout their lives.

One of the donor plaques at the Jewish cemetery on Kozma Street. Photo: Levente Tóth, 2022.

Jozefa's sister, Ilona, circa 1892.

Tuberculosis: The 19th Century White Plague

Tuberculosis, known as the white plague, was rampant in Europe. By the dawn of the 19th century, it was said to have killed one in seven of all people who had lived. Although it was thought to be hereditary, sanitoriums sprang up with the theory that fresh mountain air and sunshine were helpful in controlling the disease. Among upper class women, tuberculosis symptoms became fashionable. Carolyn Day in her book *Consumptive Chic: A History of Fashion, Beauty and Disease*, wrote "...tuberculosis enhances those things that are already established as beautiful in women ... such as the thinness and pale skin that result from weight loss and the lack of appetite caused by the disease."

One of the photographs in the box I found was of a very thin, beautiful woman. I thought she resembled Jozefa and presumed that it was Ilona, who'd died of TB at age 29.

FAMILY TREE

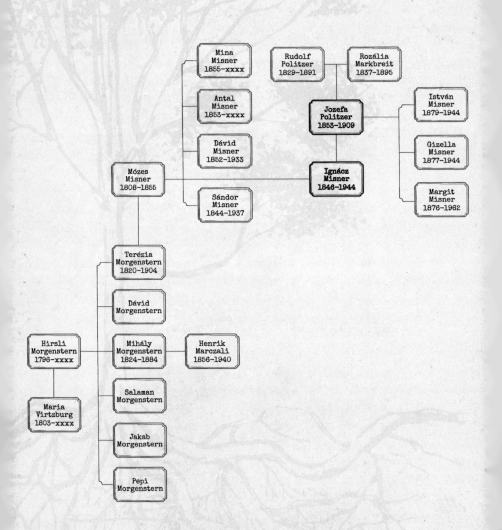

Chapter 11

Ignácz Misner

Ignácz Misner (1846-1944) married Jozefa Politzer. He was my great-great-grandfather. From humble beginnings he rose to great heights and contributed to the golden age of Hungary. Above all, he valued his family, his faith, and his loyalty to Hungary. In the end, his patriotism could not save him.

Education: Passport to Freedom

When Jozefa died, her husband Ignácz, was 63 years old and at the height of his legal career. Given the many obstacles in Ignácz's young life, his achievements were especially impressive.

He was born on May 15, 1846, in Zalaszentgrót, 135 miles southwest of Budapest. He was the second of five children born to Mózes Misner and Terézia Morgenstern. Ignácz's father, Mózes, was a livestock trader and most likely raised cows and pigs, an unexpected profession in a family that included four generations of rabbis. And not where one might expect to find the grandson of Hirsli Morgenstern – a renowned rabbi and distinguished Talmudic scholar. Ignácz's cousin, Henrik Marczali (1856-1940), was a famous historian. His book, *Hungary in the Eighteenth Century*, published in 1910 by the Cambridge University Press, was hailed in Britain as "the highest achievement of Magyar scholarship."

Education was important to this family of rabbis and scholars, but events made the attainment of education challenging. In 1855, when Ignácz was nine years old, his father and his grandfathers died in a cholera epidemic. Ignácz had to work to support himself and his family, and, according to his letter (see **Yellow Star Houses and Ignácz's Letter of Exemption on page 159**) he experienced much "toil and destitution."

From destitution in Zalaszentgrót, how did Ignácz become one the highest taxpayers in Budapest in the late 1920s and early 1930s? Education and hard work fueled his ascent. At nineteen, in 1865, he received a scholarship to attend the Lutheran Lyceum in Sopron, in northwestern Hungary. There for two years, the school had a major impact on his life. Such was his gratitude, that years later, in 1915, he established a foundation to pay the tuitions of both Christian and Jewish students at the school.

In correspondence with the school director, Ignácz wrote,

> ... your much-valued letter deeply moved me. It reminded me of the dedicated and enthusiastic education that was provided for all the students, including myself, by our beloved, respected and unforgettable teachers. I have never forgotten the magnanimous work they carried out, and whenever I had the opportunity, I talked about that really fine spirit in which the main secondary school was governed and in which it must be governed these days, as well.

Founding Member of the Budapest Bar

Following three years in law school in Vienna, Ignácz completed his studies at the University of Pest. He took the lawyer's oath on May 27, 1872. At the time there was no bar exam, as the Bar Association was established after 1875.

On October 25, 1934, the Budapest Bar celebrated its oldest members, of which Ignácz was the third oldest, having practiced for 62 years. *The Hungarian Gazette*, *The Evening*, and *The Hungarian National Reporter* were among the papers that published his interviews. One journalist described the interview setting as follows: "Dr. Misner sits in his office on the first floor of the old mansion in Terézváros. Amidst the machinegun-like rattling of typewriters, he dictates some complicated contract in a fast pace and only after expressing great reluctance is he willing to tell us something about the last 62 years." Another journalist described him as, "having a lot of vitality... he is still a young man; he is only 88 years old. His steps and speaking are graceful."

Studying in Vienna and Budapest, Ignácz understood the complicated legal structures born of the Austro-Hungarian Compromise of 1867. The resulting Dual Monarchy gave partial sovereignty and status to Hungary.

In response to the interviewer's question about university life in his school days, Ignácz replied,

> *The curriculum was much more limited than today, because there were fewer laws and they could only be amended by (royal) decrees. However, this lesser material had to be absorbed really well. At the time lawyers only studied. There were no youth organizations, no political organizations, no religious protests. The national agenda was always developing so there was nothing to protest for.*

In 1900, for the 25th anniversary of the Budapest Bar Association, the newspaper, *Country World*, published pictures of founding members. Ignácz Misner is in the second row to the far left.

He went on to describe,

> *...professors' nasty questions were unknown in university. One had to know the laws well, but those who did could surely pass the exam. Later, I myself was also an interrogator at the university...*

Ignácz started his career as a junior lawyer at the Stiller law firm. He was very dedicated, as illustrated by the story he told. Late one evening a couple of gentlemen arrived at the office wanting to set up a large shareholding company. The matter was urgent, and Dr. Stiller promised to present the drafts the next morning. However, Stiller had another urgent matter and left the preparation of this important case to Ignácz. He worked all night long to complete the Articles of Association and all the other necessary documents. Everything was handwritten, as there were no typewriters at the time.

Reading this, I was reminded of the story of Ábrahám when he impressed his uncle with his writing skills. And I thought of my father working late into the night on medical papers and grants. He would lose track of time, focused on finishing the job at hand.

Ignácz soon set up his own office and the clients came.

> *Because we lived in the Astro-Hungarian monarchy there were a lot of foreign clients. The clients came from Croatia, Romania, Serbia and Poland, and a lot of Czechs and Moravians visited my office... My private practice was quite diverse. Commerce, bill of exchange, inheritance, land, contracts... Budapest was being built during that time. The property business was booming, and we had to prepare a lot of contracts. The lawyers were doing really well.*

He went on to recount,

> *I have never been a criminal lawyer. But I had interesting cases in my career. There were big lawsuits of railway constructions, lawsuits of fire insurance worth hundreds of thousands of Pengo...No, I cannot mention any names. A lawyer is bound by full confidentiality even after this much time.*

"Of course, there were interesting civil lawsuits at that time, but the public was always interested in criminal suits," Ignácz explained. The big criminal suit of Ignácz's time was the Tiszaeszlár Blood Libel, in which his colleague, Károly Eötvös (1842-1914), defended the accused. The story was as follows: in 1883, following the disappearance of a young peasant girl, fifteen

Jewish people were accused of ritual murder on trumped-up charges and tried. The case was widely covered in the European press, which sided with the accused and where it was treated with incredulity for this "medieval feudalistic" recrimination against Jews. Thanks to the adept defense of Károly Eötvös, the accused were acquitted one year later. In the trial's aftermath, violent anti-Jewish riots erupted in numerous cities and towns lasting over two months. They led to the founding of the National Antisemitic Party. Eventually, the economic upswing at the end of the 1880s helped "chill the feverish antisemitism" and the party disappeared in the 1892 elections.

The established Jewish community in Hungary did little to respond. They placed their trust in the liberal Hungarian government of Kálmán Tisza. Young intellectuals, Jews and non-Jews, campaigned to legislate Judaism as equal to other religions in Hungary. In 1895, the Law of Reception (Law XLII) passed, making Judaism a state-endorsed religion, equal to Christianity. It was the outcome of a larger culture war waged between 1892 and 1895 in parliament on the separation of church and state.

Love: Family and Country

The established Jewish community was deeply and genuinely pro-Magyar. This allegiance was expressed in the promotion of the Hungarian language. The Dohány Synagogue, a Neolog (reform) synagogue, decided that the community leaders should be enlightened rabbis capable of delivering their sermons not only in Hebrew, but also in Hungarian in order to educate the younger Jewish generation.

Ignácz was an ardent Hungarian patriot in every way. He had named his children: Margit, Gizella, and István after the royal family of the House of Árpád, Hungary's founding fathers. He was also active in the Jewish community and served on the board of the Jewish Territorial Organization, established for creating a "national home for the Jewish people."

In 1893, he wrote an article in the Jewish religious and societal weekly, *Equality*, proposing the establishment of a foundation to spread the Hungarian language among Jews who did not speak Hungarian, in preparation for the Millennium celebration of 1896. Jews typically spoke two languages,

Yiddish and the language of their native home: Slovakia, Galicia, Romania, Serbia, Croatia, and Germany. Almost half of the total population in the Hungarian lands of the Austro-Hungarian empire did not speak Hungarian.

András, who translated the article, described it as eloquent: "This man must have spoken so beautifully if he could write so beautifully!" Ignácz wrote,

> The unity of the language makes the citizens a nation: the unified language is a shared treasure that all members of the nation are ready to protect with devotion; the unity of the language makes the citizens brothers and sisters, and it leads to ease the tensions among the various denominations. The unity of the language provides bigger power, stronger self-esteem for the nation and ensures its existence till the end of times... If I created an ideal for myself about the future of Hungary, the unity of the Hungarian language would take the first place.

When Ignácz wrote his article on the unity of language in 1893, Hungary was in the midst of the national euphoria that led up to the Millennium celebrations in 1896. The Millennium was to be Hungary's greatest celebration, demonstrating the achievement of its manifest destiny as a country, even within the framework of the Dual Monarchy. Hungarians were determined to outdo Chicago's 1893 world exposition. The Millennium celebration was to be Hungary's and Budapest's worldwide debut.

Paul Lendvai, in his book, *The Hungarians: A Thousand Years of Victory in Defeat*, described the opening of the Millennium celebrations in May 1896. "There were balls, receptions, and celebrations all over the country." The Jewish newspapers reported that on the morning of May 9th, 8,000 Jewish men and women attended a service at the Dohány Synagogue, dressed in tailcoats and elegant dresses.

> The first rows were filled with government representatives, ennobled magnates, well-known bankers and industrialists; most wore full-dress, uniforms with dolmans thrown over their shoulders, jeweled trimmings, egret plumes, sabers and boots with gold or silver spurs.

Their elaborate costumes were a symbol of Magyar pride and nationalism. I could imagine that Ignácz and Jozefa would have been in attendance to celebrate.

By the time of the Millennium celebrations, Ignácz and Jozefa's three children were young adults, two had their own apartments in Ignácz's home. Ignácz had selected Nagykörút, the Grand Boulevard, (see **Budapest Becomes a Sophisticated Cosmopolitan Center on page 157**) to build a grand home where he moved his family in 1888.

They were actively involved in the Jewish community, with seats at the Dohány Synagogue. These seats were so expensive and highly prized that there was a saying among the local Jewish community, "members of the congregation should possess an apartment, a weekend house, and a seat in the Dohány Street Synagogue." They possessed all three. In 1917, Ignácz bought a villa on Sváb Hill, the tallest of the Buda Hills. He already owned a large working farm in Ercsi (purchased in 1897), about one hour south of Budapest.

Not only was his law practice flourishing, but Ignácz, together with several of the Politzers, invested in real estate and profited from the construction boom. According to KÉK, an independent architectural cultural center, "The Politzer family .... was one of the largest purchasers of the plots along Teréz körút."

Ignácz built his home on Teréz körút 45, where my father grew up. Zsigmond was across the street at #47, Ármin (Móricz's son) owned #32 and #17, though he lived at Andrássy út 17. Gusztáv owned #25 though he lived in a mansion on Bulyovszky street (currently Rippl Rónai), and Bernát lived at #5. At least four of the apartment buildings were designed by Henrik Schmahl, among the first architects in Budapest to combine commercial and residential blocks, where the ground floor was dedicated to shops and businesses and separated from the residential upper stories.

As was typical of that time, Ignácz moved his law office to their home on Teréz körút 45, the site of his 1934 interview celebrating him as one of the oldest members of the Hungarian Bar. When the interviewer asked Ignácz what he was proud of, he responded:

> *There is nothing to be proud of if one served justice loyally and to the best of his knowledge for 62 years... If there is anything to be*

proud of in the past 62 years it can only be that a lot of sworn enemies met in my office and left peacefully, without a lawsuit, because I always believed that those who file a lawsuit are angry, and those who are angry are not right, so first and foremost one has to establish reconciliation between the parties... Believe me, if there is anything I can be proud of, then I am proud of the cases which were settled with a friendly handshake in my office.

I have gathered the experience from the years spent with endless work that times are changing, people are changing, and laws are also changing. One thing never changes and will never change till the end of time: eternal truth. I could perhaps be proud of this fact that I have always fought for justice.

Eternal truth. Justice. I felt so proud to be his great-great-granddaughter. So glad I had found him. I teared up reading his final words from that interview:

The legacy of a long life and practice...? I am happiest when I am in my villa on Sváb-hill with my two great-grandchildren, working in my orchard. My great-grandchild may once become a lawyer, as did his father, grandfather and great-grandfather. I planted my fruit trees myself, I grafted them all myself and I trim them myself every year. And my trees have their precious yields every year. I did not plant and take care of them in vain. I think hard work always pays off. Perhaps I did not serve justice for so many years for nothing...

My father occasionally referred to his great-grandfather, bragging that he worked until the age of 99. When Ignácz showed signs of dementia, his son István, now in charge of his law practice, fictionalized law cases for his father to work on so that he could feel productive in the office.

Ignácz Misner's house at Teréz körút 45.

Teréz körút 32 owned by Ármin Politzer, Jozefa's cousin.

Inside courtyard of Gusztáv Politzer's house at Teréz körút 25. Gusztáv was Jozefa's uncle.

Bernát Politzer lived at Teréz körút 5. Bernát was Jozefa's uncle.

All is Lost

During World War II, Ignácz was robbed of many of his honors and professional achievements. On January 31, 1939, Ignácz was removed from the Directory of Attorneys. The reason given: his inability to work and earn. He was almost 93 and starting to show signs of dementia. The Numerus Clausus acts also factored into the decision to publicly remove him. The first act, passed in May 1938, two months after the Anschluss (the annexation of Austria into Nazi Germany), restricted the number of Jewish lawyers to 20%. It is estimated that the law deprived 400,000 Jewish lawyers, doctors, and other professionals of their jobs and livelihood.

On September 6, 1942, a fourth decree was passed confiscating Jewish farmland. All persons classified as Jewish had to hand over their land, their forests, their tools, and their animals. In 1943, Ignácz's beloved farm in Ercsi was expropriated. By the end of 1943, 751,000 acres of farmland and forestry assets owned by Jews were confiscated.

On August 17, 1943, which would have been Ignácz and Jozefa's 68th wedding anniversary, Ignácz asked Istók, the gardener at their villa, to gather a bouquet of flowers to visit Jozefa's grave. Nothing, not even the Arrow Cross thugs, could keep him away from this dangerous trip to the Jewish cemetery. His granddaughter Lili accompanied him so he would not go alone.

In March 1944, the Germans occupied Hungary. More ruthless decrees were introduced each day. In early April, a decree banning all Jews from employing a Christian at their workplace or in their homes, compelled Ignácz to dismiss his loyal housekeeper of 27 years (though she continued to help the family, smuggling in food and messages). By the end of April, Jews had to turn in all their gold objects. Gábor Virány wrote, "Old Ignácz could not be held back from personally delivering his cherished golden pocket watch which he wore for several decades."

I could imagine my great-great-grandfather, 98 years old, marching down to Gestapo headquarters to turn in his watch. Nobody could intimidate him. With his strong sense of justice, he would have wanted to look

Ignácz Misner with his two granddaughters, Bözsi (my grandmother) and Lili, circa 1907.

his perpetrators in the eye. Would he have tried to reconcile his differences with them, as he had with old clients?

In June 1944, Ignácz lost his home. (see **Yellow Star Houses and Ignácz's Letter of Exemption on page 159**). Due to the German invasion in March, they had already abandoned the villa at Sváb Hill. Now, the family was forced to move out of their only remaining home on Teréz körút and into a yellow star house at Személynök street No.19. Jews in Budapest were assigned to one of 2000 yellow star houses, one family per room. Similar to a ghetto, the houses served as a preparatory stage for deportation to concentration camps. The family had to leave behind all their belongings. Gábor wrote that among all of Ignácz's valuable paintings, furniture, carpets, silver and gold, the old man grieved most for the picture of his beloved wife, Jozefa.

In the box (containing the documents, letters, and photos) was a letter addressed to Governor Horthy, the Regent (leader) of Hungary, asking to be allowed to return to their home. It was signed by Ignácz. However, Gábor described in his book how István had written the letter. Ignácz's mind had been deteriorating and he was no longer capable. István knew his father's very old and respectful style and could write such a letter on Ignácz's behalf.

In September, the family received a reply to the letter. Gábor said that the letter had an impact but did not specify further. Did they receive the Governor's privilege and if so, what did that mean? Could they return to their home, which by now had been given away to others? Did they receive exemption from all the limitations? Gábor wrote, "Ignácz did not want to take off the yellow star, he wore his Judaism as a matter of pride."

The Jewish holidays were in September that year, but his daughter Margit wouldn't allow Ignácz to go to the Dohány Synagogue to celebrate. Deportations had been temporarily stopped. But it was still risky to go out. The family celebrated quietly at the yellow star house with Lili, whose Hebrew was excellent, leading the prayer.

Ignácz did not attend services at the synagogue, but not because he feared for his life. The real reason: "The congregation was without a spiritual leader because the celebrated rabbi, Simon Hevesi, died in February (1943)," Gábor wrote. Dr. Hevesi was a noted scholar, prolific

Ignácz Misner wearing his gold watch, circa 1930.

author, and brilliant speaker. He had become chief rabbi of Pest in 1927. He was responsible for the development of Jewish culture and education throughout Hungary and active in welfare and religious organizations. He had been a friend of the family.

On October 15, 1944, when Horthy announced Hungary's withdrawal from the war, the Arrow Cross (the Hungarian Nazis) seized power with military help from the Germans. The new regime would not accept the former exemptions. István's letter had been in vain.

Life became even more dangerous and precarious. Margit secured a place for Ignácz in an elderly care home on Géllert Hill. Ignácz's advancing dementia was problematic and made his care challenging. The home could not handle him and sent him to a home opposite the entrance of the Jewish ghetto. On December 23rd, some distant relatives found him wandering the streets and took him to the hospital in the ghetto.

On December 27th, a mere 10 years after Ignácz was celebrated as a founding member of the Hungarian Bar, he died from starvation in the hospital in the Jewish ghetto. He had lost everything.

In addition, according to the Chevra Kadisha Budapest, he is buried in the mass grave (row IV. No.3a) of the Jewish Cemetery in Kerepesi street, Budapest. Despite many attempts, Margit was unable to transfer his body to the family crypt. Only his name is engraved there.

Ignácz's name is on the Misner Family Tombstone: Crypt No 43 (L) at the Kozma Street Cemetery, Budapest, Hungary. His body was buried in a mass grave in the Jewish section of the Kerepesi Cemetery, Budapest. Photo: Levente Tóth, 2022.

LEARNING MORE

Budapest Becomes a Sophisticated Cosmopolitan Center

The Jewish Emancipation Act of 1868 gave Jews equality before the law and eliminated barriers to their participation in the economy. Hungary became home to the second-largest Jewish population on the continent, with almost a million Jewish citizens on the eve of World War I. Although there were conflicts within the Jewish population (between the Orthodox Jews and the newly formed Neologs), a significant proportion of Hungarian Jews zealously identified with Hungarian nationalism, becoming assimilated in Hungarian language and culture. Jews were leaders in the development of capitalism in Hungary. They were bankers, financiers, and merchants. They also became lawyers, doctors, architects, and journalists. And continued to expand Hungary's agricultural base as managers and owners of large and medium-sized estates. As Jews attained prominent positions in a wide variety of walks of life, assimilation, including many interfaith marriages, was widespread.

In 1873, Buda, Pest, and Óbuda merged to become Budapest. The Dual Monarchy invested heavily in the development of the city. Budapest became not just a capital, but the Hungarian capital, with a castle for the king and the awe-inspiring Parliament building (built 1885-1904). Massive development commenced, including the building of monuments and museums.

City planners modeled boulevards and parks after Paris and Vienna. Nagykörút (the Grand Boulevard) was the largest of four semi-circle boulevards and became the dynamic center of the city. Nagykörút is the collective name for five linked streets, or sections of the boulevard, which were named after the Habsburg monarchs: Szent István körút, Teréz körút, Erzsébet körút, József körút and Ferenc körút.

Nagykörút was the first to establish an electricity network. Tram traffic began in 1887. Flanked by buildings designed by renowned architects, it was a showcase for a modern city thoroughfare.

In 1896, an electrified subway system was completed, only the second such line in Europe (after Britain) to connect the city center to the city park.

Budapest became a sophisticated cosmopolitan city – a center of intellectual energy, cultural advancements, technological achievements, and financial expansion. In practically every field, from music to nuclear physics, Austro-Hungarians were leaders. Gathering with people of like mind to exchange ideas, they met at the university and at the salons and cafés that flourished in Budapest. And for the first time, Jews with the talent and ambition to achieve could be part of the conversation.

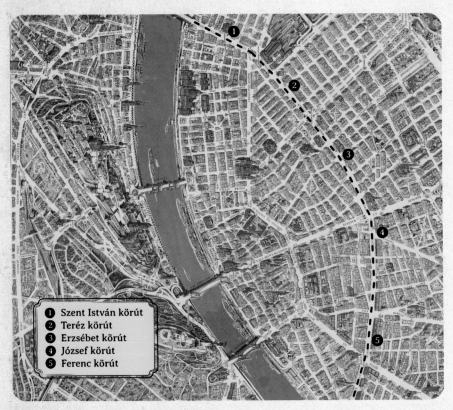

1. Szent István körút
2. Teréz körút
3. Erzsébet körút
4. József körút
5. Ferenc körút

Nagykörút (the Grand Boulevard) connects Margaret bridge on the north and Petőfi Bridge on the south. Teréz körút is the 2nd section running from the Nyugati train station (built by Eiffel) to the street beyond Andrássy Avenue. / Budapest City Archives.

Yellow Star Houses and Ignácz's Letter of Exemption

Among the documents found in the box my sister rescued from my parents' home after the fire was a letter written in June 1944 by Ignácz Misner to Miklós Horthy, the Regent of Hungary. When Anna Bayer translated it, my family came to life, as she enriched their stories with historical context.

I knew nothing about the "Yellow Star Houses," unique to Budapest in the history of the Holocaust. Anna explained that in June 1944, all Jewish citizens, already ordered to wear the yellow star, were forcibly relocated to designated houses marked with a yellow star. There were almost 2,000 such residences throughout the city, accommodating an estimated 220,000 people. Each family was allowed one room. This mass relocation was to prepare them for deportation to concentration camps.

In the letter, Ignácz requested an exemption for his family from the mandatory restrictive measures placed on Jews. He begins:

> *To justify my most humble request, I permit myself to present to you that I was born in Zalaszentgrót on the 15th day of May 1846 and so I am now 99 years of age. By a special grace of God, I reached this high age fully in command of my mental and physical capabilities and I became the eldest attorney-at-law in the country.*

He went on to describe how his father died of cholera when he was two. (Later we found out that Ignácz's son István wrote the letter. He was mistaken when he wrote that Ignácz was two when his father died. His correct age was nine.) Ignácz worked to support himself from the age of nine. After much "toil and destitution" he earned his law degree and practiced for 67 years, until 1939 when he was forced to retire. He was very active on various legal committees and published many legal papers.

There has never been a disciplinary complaint lodged against me... I have never been engaged in political matters, I have never been a member of any political party, let alone of a lodge of free masons. I devoted all my life to my work, a major part of which constituted the pro bono administration of cases for the poor. I have always been guided by patriotism and national sentiment of which I have never been diverted.

He continued, describing how he had to leave his home of 60 years. He repeated that no family members were ever members of political parties or the lodge of free masons. He concludes:

As an old man I can hardly reconcile myself with this horrific situation, in which I landed through no fault of my own.

With Anna's help, I found the yellow-star house, approximately a 20-minute walk from their home on Teréz körút. On Google maps we could see a picture of the house today. On the website yellowstarhouses. org, we read testimonies from residents of the houses, harrowing stories of mothers, children, and the elderly alone (the men were called up for forced labor service), facing constant harassment and abuse by the Arrow Cross while trying to survive deprivation and starvation.

In the box we found lists, inventories, of what they took with them and what was left behind. Anna explained how the decrees forced Jews to abandon most of their cherished belongings. Much of what they were forced to abandon was stolen by other Hungarian citizens, Nazis or the Arrow Cross soldiers. Ignácz's list of what he took to the yellow star house included 8 pairs of underwear, 1 dressing gown, 8 shirts, 7 suits, 1 winter coat, 1 pair winter boots, 1 summer coat, 3 pairs of shoes, 12 pairs of socks, 14 pocket handkerchiefs, a bed and mattress, 5 large pillows, 1 quilt, 6 bed sheets, 1 night table, 1 lamp, 1 towel, 1 umbrella, 1 walking stick, a pipe and tobacco, and 5 books. He had to leave behind the painting of his beloved Jozefa.

The yellow star house. In June 1944, the extended family was forced to inhabit one room there. Photo 2019.

FAMILY TREE

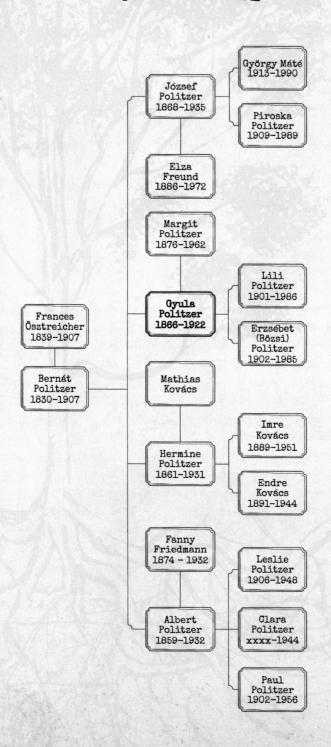

György Máté
1913-1990

Piroska
Politzer
1909-1989

József
Politzer
1868-1935

Elza
Freund
1886-1972

Margit
Politzer
1876-1962

Lili
Politzer
1901-1986

Gyula
Politzer
1866-1922

Erzsébet
(Bözsi)
Politzer
1902-1985

Frances
Ösztreicher
1839-1907

Mathias
Kovács

Bernát
Politzer
1830-1907

Imre
Kovács
1889-1951

Hermine
Politzer
1861-1931

Endre
Kovács
1891-1944

Fanny
Friedmann
1874 - 1932

Leslie
Politzer
1906-1948

Clara
Politzer
xxxx-1944

Albert
Politzer
1859-1932

Paul
Politzer
1902-1956

Chapter 12

Gyula Politzer

Gyula Politzer (1866-1922) was the son of Francis (Fanny) Ösztreicher and Bernát Politzer (1830-1907), Ábrahám and Caroline's sixth son. Gyula married his niece, Margit, the daughter of Jozefa and Ignácz Misner. Gyula was my great-grandfather. The only thing I knew about him before embarking on the search that became this book was that my father, Julian, was named after him.

The Wedding Invitation

A joyous day occurred for Ignácz and Jozefa Misner on May 27, 1900. That date marked their eldest daughter's marriage. Simon Hevesi, Ignácz's favorite rabbi and a highly respected individual in the community, officiated at the wedding of Margit Misner and Gyula Politzer at the Dohány Synagogue, the second largest synagogue in the world. I imagine it was a grand celebration. Illés, Ádám and Zsigmond would have been there with their spouses, children (Jozefa's cousins), and grandchildren. And at least sixty-five more immediate family members gathered to fete the newly-weds.

I found their elegant wedding invitation – heavy beige linen paper with feathered edges – in the box that survived my parents' house fire. Though creased and yellowed, its graceful, old-world calligraphy was lovely and still clearly legible. The invitation from Dr. Misner Ignácz (in Hungarian the last name is written first) was on the left side; the invitation that came from Politzer Bernát was on the right.

I remember being shocked when I realized that Margit had married her uncle, Gyula Politzer. Did they marry for love? Did they marry to preserve family wealth?

I knew intermarriage between royal dynasties was prevalent. There were many other examples, even those in scientific fields – Charles Darwin and Albert Einstein married their first cousins. Apparently, it was a common practice not only for Jews, but for people of all religions throughout the centuries. My shock subsided when I learned that, according to one statistic, today 20% of all couples worldwide are first cousins.

Gyula Politzer was 34 years old, ten years Margit's senior when they married in 1900. We don't know when and how Margit and Gyula fell in love, but in *Our Family History*, Zsigmond wrote that Gyula and Margit's marriage was a happy one.

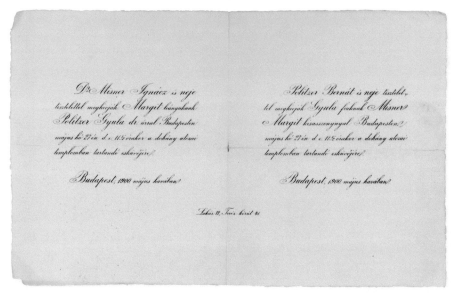

Margit and Gyula's Wedding Invitation. May 27, 1900.

Margit and Gyula, circa 1900.

Kindhearted and Trustworthy

Gyula was my father's grandfather. Gyula is Hungarian for Julian, my father's name. Other than that single fact, no one talked about him. I wished my grandmother Bözsi, Gyula's daughter, had shared her memories. From what I learned, I imagined him radiating love and comforting those he touched.

Gyula was born on December 9, 1866, in Kecskemét, a city 55 miles southeast of Budapest. He was the third child of Bernát and Fanny Politzer. (see **Bernát and Fanny: True Love and Devotion on page 172**) He was close to his siblings: Albert, seven years older, became a successful businessman and had three children, one of whom died in the Holocaust. Gyula most cherished his sister, Hermine, five years older. Of her two sons (Imre and Endre Kovács), my father's favorite uncles, one died in Auschwitz and the other shortly after the war (see **Chapter 12**). József, seven years younger, had two children and two grandchildren. His grandchildren, György and Zsuzsanna Máté currently live in Budapest.

My newly found cousins, György Máté and his sister Zsuzsanna Méniet.

Though the family was observant and kept kosher, they sent their sons to Roman Catholic grammar school. I could only surmise that Gyula attended Catholic school because it was the best academic institution of the time.

Until 7th grade (the equivalent of 11th grade in the US), Gyula attended the same school his father and uncles – Illés, Rudolf, and Ádám – had attended. He mostly received "excellent" grades, with a few "fairs" dimming his record. When they moved to Budapest in 1883, Gyula attended the Calvinist grammar school in Budapest for his last year of gymnasium (the equivalent of high school). At the end of the school year, friends from the class wrote an agreement that they would meet again in 10 years in May 1894. I don't know if the reunion ever occurred. However, I was impressed that Gyula, who had only been there a year, had made friends so quickly.

In 1888, at the age of 22, Gyula received his law certificate from the Law Faculty of the Royal Hungarian University of Science in Budapest. A student went directly to medical school or law school following graduation from gymnasium, different from the educational systems of today. Five years later, following the accepted course for a young lawyer, the Budapest Bar listed him as one of the trainee lawyers. Eventually he became general counsel for Kőbánya Savings Bank.

In *Our Family History*, Zsigmond described Gyula as "loyal, sincere, kind-hearted and most like his father, while he had the modesty and forbearance of his mother. His trustworthiness and appreciation earned him the vote of the whole family to become President of the Háy Fund." (see **The Háy Fund: A Tradition of Altruism on page 173**).

Gyula's portrait suggests a gentle soulfulness. With that twinkle in his eye and a smile, accentuated by his large, upturned mustache, he seemed playfully roguish. I imagined him to be gregarious and popular like his father.

Photo of a portrait of Gyula Politzer. Photo found in box in my parents' home.

A Charmed Life

The new century began as a flourishing time for Hungarian Jews, especially in Budapest. Economic expansion, social mobility, and exuberant hope characterized the early years before World War I. Gyula and Margit's family grew with the arrival of two daughters. Lili was born on September 24, 1901. A year and four days later (September 28, 1902), my grandmother Erzsébet (Bözsi for short) was born.

Several pictures and postcards, found in the box, depicted happy family vacations. Trieste, Venice, and Lake Balaton were popular destinations, but most favored was Abbazia (currently Opatija, Croatia). At the head of the Fiume gulf, Abbazia was considered an equal rival to the Bay of Naples for its "beauty and picturesqueness," according to an 1888 travel magazine.

Frederic Morton, in *A Nervous Splendor, Vienna 1888/1889*, described chic Abbazia as "The Monarchy's Cannes on the Adriatic." I wondered if Gyula and Margit saw Emperor Franz Joseph and Empress Sisi. It was a place to rub shoulders with members of the imperial family, celebrities, diplomats, the cream of society, as well as artists and writers. A place of grand hotels, luxurious resorts, sailing, horse racing, fine dining, and elegant balls. A place for those fortunate enough to lead a charmed life.

The turn of the century was a time of economic expansion and social mobility, but it was also a time that brought "seeds of trouble," as described by John Lukacs in his book, *Budapest 1900*. Rifts arose in economic standing, social class, and political, religious and geopolitical thinking – capitalism versus socialism, the landed gentry versus the working class, liberal versus conservative, Christian versus Jew, nationalism versus multiculturalism. Reading his descriptions, I was disturbed by its ominous parallels to our world today.

In a "symbolic coincidence," on July 23, 1914, the entire sky above Budapest burst open into a tornado. One hundred mile per hour winds destroyed buildings, tore off the roof of the Basilica, damaged the Chain Bridge and

Postcard from Abbazia. Lili and Bözsi in 1906.

Gizella, Margit's sister, with Lili and Bözsi. At Lake Balaton, circa 1905.

brought deaths and many injuries. It was without precedent, as John Lukacs went on to describe. Two days later, Austria-Hungary broke off relations with Serbia, and thus began World War I.

Gyula was 48 years old when World War I broke out, too old to enlist or be called to war. However, Margit volunteered as a nurse (see **Chapter 13**), and many nephews joined the fight.

A Young Widow

Hungary emerged from the ashes of World War I, having lost two-thirds of its territory and two-thirds of its citizens. The country was rocked by economic and political instability. In search of a scapegoat, Jews became targets despite having fought valiantly in the war. In the minds of many Hungarians, Jews were often seen to be at the root of Hungary's fall. In September 1920, the government passed the first Numerus Clausus, a law that limited the number of Jewish university students to 6%.

The anxiety and stress that the Politzer family experienced most likely had profound consequences. On June 10, 1922, at the age of 56, Gyula died. The cause: heart disease. His death left a deep void. Margit never remarried. Together with Margit, his two daughters, Lili and Bözsi, visited his grave every year.

Their devotion was so strong, that even in 1943, Bözsi insisted on visiting his grave, despite Margit's fear and protests. Many violent antisemitic incidents made riding the bus to the cemetery risky. But Bözsi was adamant that she would honor her father and visit his grave.

Gyula Politzer, circa 1915.

LEARNING MORE

Bernát and Fanny: True Love

Zsigmond Politzer wrote in *Our Family History* that Gyula was most like his father, Bernát: loyal, sincere, kindhearted and trustworthy. Bernát was the sixth child of Ábrahám and Karoline Politzer. He was named after their rabbi, who died in the cholera epidemic a few days before Bernát was born in 1830 (see **Chapter 5**). According to Zsigmond, Bernát was sensitive and hard-working. He was an avid reader. His level-headed demeanor and special way with people, "won him many friends."

In 1856, Bernát married Fanny Ösztreicher, the daughter of a businessman and real estate owner. Fanny, serious and quiet, was the perfect complement to Bernát's gregariousness.

Bernát and Fanny Politzer.

They were devoted to one another. Zsigmond recounted, "Fanny and Bernát lived in harmony and happily for over 50 years. It is said that they never had a single argument. Their love was so deep that she only outlived him by a mere two months, even though she was not ill at all." They died in 1907.

The Háy Fund: A Tradition of Altruism

In the mid 19th-century, Gyula's great-great-grandfather, Zelig Háy, established the Háy Fund. Many of the Politzer/Háy family's philanthropic activities throughout the next century were supported by this fund.

In 1896, Dr. Béla Vajda, Rabbi of Abony, wrote a book, *The History of the Jews in and around Abony*. About Zelig Háy, Gyula's great-great-grandfather, he wrote, "From the beginning of this century (1800s) he has been a caring father not only to his big family but to the whole Jewish community. He is a real guardian of the poor, and the majority of the congregation is poor. He gives a dole for the hungry; he helps those who are able to work to get their food. When the Jewish community ran out of funding, the old Zelig was always there, and either loaned or donated the necessary amount."

Of Jakab Háy, Zelig's son and Gyula's great-grandfather, the rabbi wrote, "This noble-minded man set up Kaddish endowments in the amount of 400 forints for the local, as well as the Jerusalem, Kecskemét, Irsa, Törökszentmiklós, Tiszabeő, Bicske, Leipnik and other Jewish communities. In his final will he left a large family foundation for dowry purposes and other charitable causes. Furthermore, he commemorated the Pest Jewish Women's Association, the Institute of the Blind, the local Jewish, Roman Catholic and Protestant public schools."

Zelig had started a foundation worth 10,000 guilders for the poor. Jakab expanded the foundation. Upon Jakab's death the foundation was managed by Pest County and Bernát, Gyula's father, was its president. Later it was taken over by the Jewish Community in Abony and Gyula was named President of the Háy Fund.

FAMILY TREE

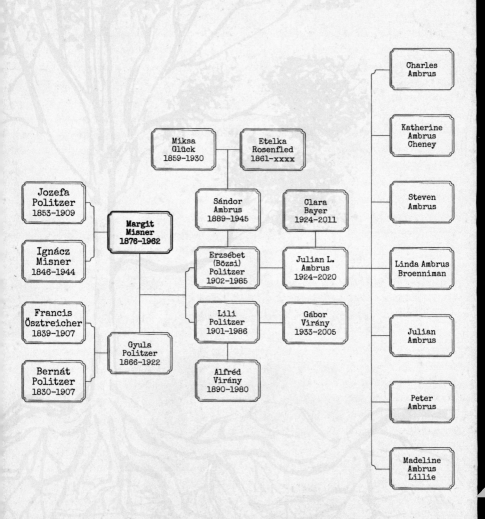

Miksa Glück 1859–1930

Etelka Rosenfled 1861–xxxx

Jozefa Politzer 1853–1909

Ignácz Misner 1846–1944

Margit Misner 1876–1962

Francis Ösztreicher 1839–1907

Bernát Politzer 1830–1907

Gyula Politzer 1866–1922

Sándor Ambrus 1889–1945

Erzsébet (Bözsi) Politzer 1902–1985

Lili Politzer 1901–1986

Alfréd Virány 1890–1980

Clara Bayer 1924–2011

Julian L. Ambrus 1924–2020

Gábor Virány 1933–2005

Charles Ambrus

Katherine Ambrus Cheney

Steven Ambrus

Linda Ambrus Broenniman

Julian Ambrus

Peter Ambrus

Madeline Ambrus Lillie

Chapter 13

Margit Misner Politzer

Growing up, I knew nothing about my great-grandfather, Gyula Politzer. And only small bits and pieces about his wife, Margit Misner Politzer (1876-1962), my great-grandmother. In a revelatory moment, my sister's godmother described Margit as the grand dame of the family. "Like all Jewish mothers, she ruled the roost," she said. Until that moment in my late 20s, neither I nor my siblings knew that we had a Jewish great-grandmother – or that my father's family was Jewish.

Indomitable Spirit

Margit was 32 when her mother, Jozefa, died, and she took responsibility for multiple households – her father's, her brother's, and later her two daughters'. After she became a widow, at age 46, she no longer went on extravagant vacations. She was busy at home. She managed all the servants at Teréz körút, the summer villa at Sváb Hill and the farm in Ercsi. She often had to placate those who were upset by her father's and brother's demanding perfectionism. She organized social events, teas, dinners and parties for family, friends, and important clients.

Margit especially loved the family villa on Sváb Hill, located in the Buda Hills, and its extensive formal gardens. She took great joy in her flowers. Her appreciation for the beauty in life extended to art. Like Margit's cousin, Albert, and nephew, Rudi, (see **Chapter 9**), her uncle Ádám inspired her. She became a passionate collector of paintings, sketches, antique furniture, and other objects of art. She often consulted with Rudi when acquiring pieces for her collection.

I learned much of this from my father in our weekly phone conversations during the last years of his life. When I asked him what he remembered most about Margit, his grandmother, he paused, overcome with emotion. His voice trembled, "She was the most kind and generous person I will ever know.

Everyone, young and old, ran to her to solve their problems – all sorts of big and small problems."

I remembered stories my mother had told me about how Margit would open her home once a week to welcome those in need of jobs, medical care, food, or money. She tried to help however she could: calling on her wealthy friends to seek out employment opportunities, paying doctor's bills and school tuition for those who couldn't afford it, and sending food and money home with those who petitioned her.

Margit was active in the Pest Jewish Women's Association, founded in 1866. Typical of Margit, she was part of this philanthropic organization, which opened orphanages and shelters for poor women. It opened the first soup kitchen in 1869. At the outbreak of World War I, its soup kitchens served over 280,000 people per year.

World War I and Its Aftermath

Margit trained as a nurse volunteer and went to work for the Red Cross taking care of World War I victims. She saw devastating physical injuries and brutal emotional damage and did not shy away from helping those who were wounded and suffering. Several of Margit's cousins and nephews who fought returned with physical and emotional scars, despite being decorated officers. I imagine she attended to them as she had to many other soldiers.

After World War I, between 1919 and 1921, revolutionary and counter-revolutionary violence swept through Hungary (see **Chaos and Antisemitic Violence in the Aftermath of World War I on page 199**). Paramilitary gangs unleashed terror. A notably sadistic paramilitary unit was headquartered next to Margit's Teréz körút home in the Hotel Britannia. They used blackmail and extortion to prey on rich Jewish businessmen, who were kidnapped, tortured, and executed if they refused to pay.

I had known nothing about this dark period in Hungarian history. Margit's father, husband, and brother could have been prime targets. Living next door to the hotel, they must have feared such a fate. We know they survived this grim period, but they did suffer other losses.

Margit, with her two daughters, Lili and Bözsi (my grandmother), circa 1904.

The 1920 Treaty of Trianon, which formally ended World War I, forced Hungary to cede two thirds of its former territory. The Politzer landholdings in the newly formed Yugoslavia were seized. According to my father, the family had discovered a large quarry on a property they had purchased for its excellent boar hunting. A marble mine was built and became a significant source of family wealth during the construction boom of the late 19th century. The mine, too, was confiscated.

After several years of legal proceedings over the confiscated mine, Margit used the restitution money, only a minute fraction of the property's value, to buy my father a film projector and some movies.

Margit as a volunteer nurse during WWI. She is second from left in the top row.

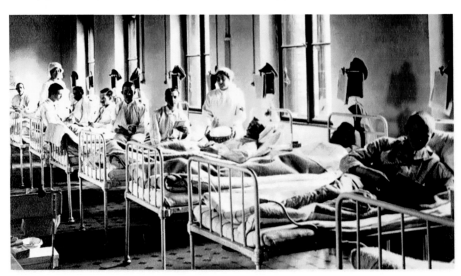

Margit behind a patient in the third bed from the right.

The Interwar Years

In *Budapest 1900*, author John Lukacs wrote about the interwar years, "Hungarians have an instinctive genius for recovery after their worst disasters... People in Budapest breathed freer. The air became lighter." (see **Recovery After World War I on page 201**).

Margit's younger daughter, Bözsi, (my grandmother), married Sándor Ambrus (my grandfather) on January 14, 1923. They moved into the apartment adjacent to Margit's. In 1931, Lili, Margit's older daughter, married Alfréd Virány and moved to an apartment on the top floor. After my father was born in 1924, Margit became a second mother to him, as Bözsi and Sándor were busy entertaining clients and friends.

The family prospered once again. In 1927 and 1928 Margit's father, Ignácz, became one of the highest taxpayers in Budapest. In 1927, Margit bought a home (the family's fourth) in Vienna. The house, on Walfischgasse, was one block from the Opera House, one block from the Hotel Sacher, and close to major museums. I wonder if Margit bought this house because of her fond memories of spending time in Vienna with her great uncles Ádám and Zsigmond, who'd died in the early 1920s. My father described how, as a young boy, they used to spend the "opera season" in Vienna, attending the opening balls, going to museums, shopping, and his favorite activity, watching the Lipizzaner's (the white horses of the Spanish Riding School of Vienna, famous for their beauty and athletic ability).

World War II

Margit survived World War I, the White Terror, the aftermath of the Treaty of Trianon, and the death of her husband. But the years between 1923 and 1938 were merely a pause in the succession of catastrophes that would upend the world and cause Margit more personal suffering.

On March 12, 1938, German troops crossed the border into Austria. The troops were greeted by cheering Austrians with Nazi salutes and Nazi flags. The "Anschluss," or the German annexation of Austria, received enthusiastic support from most of the Austrian population. Widespread antisemitic violence followed quickly.

Margit had planned a dinner party for the next day, Sunday March 13th. She loved to entertain, often hosting girlfriends for tea and their families for dinner. Margit was a socialite. using social gatherings to enhance the family's connections. But she also used her social networks to help those in need.

Her dinner party, planned for weeks, was to celebrate one of her dearest girlfriends, Paula. They had been classmates as young girls. Paula was Christian, but they had remained close. On the morning of the party, Paula phoned to express her regrets. She and her husband would be unable to attend. Others did the same, fearing for their safety as news streamed in. It seemed only a matter of time before antisemitic attacks would spread to Budapest. I imagine Margit knew that it was for the best. When Paula's husband died a few months later, she did not attend the funeral, sending a card instead.

For six years, Budapest was relatively insulated from the war. Jews were not being evicted. However, with rampant antisemitism their freedoms were severely restricted. Jews hoped that the war would end, that Budapest would survive intact, and that their lives would return to the golden days before war. They tried to go about their daily lives with that optimism. They did not imagine what the war might bring when it finally arrived on their doorstep.

The Yellow Star House and Christian Jews

In March 1944, the Germans occupied Hungary. With the legalization of the Arrow Cross, the Hungarian Nazi party, the family was no longer safe. Margit maintained her composure, organizing and directing the many moves, the first was to the yellow star house (see **Chapter 11**).

On June 16th, the mayor of Budapest issued a decree compelling all Jewish residents to move to yellow star houses before June 24th. One week later, nine family members, had to leave their spacious apartments and share a single room. Margit oversaw the packing for her family: her father Ignácz, her sister Gizella and her husband Frigyes Tibold (whose large estate outside Budapest had been confiscated in 1943), her brother István, her daughter Bözsi (whose husband and son had been sent into forced labor), and her daughter Lili's family, including Alfréd and Gábor.

To prepare for their move, they created official lists of their assets, what they were taking and what they were leaving behind. These lists had to be witnessed and given to Nazi officials.

Copies of many of these lists survived the war and were in the box rescued from my parents' home. We also found some partial lists. I presume those were "unofficial;" they included hidden items, listed because they believed they would return home.

I imagined their anguish. They were allowed to take only the minimum (clothes, beds and bed linens, towels) for survival. They packed summer and winter clothes, in anticipation of a lengthy exile. Any possessions of value had already been turned in to the Hungarian authorities. But family heirlooms, collected artwork, and other sentimental possessions that had brought them joy (but were of little real value), were left behind.

István Dobó, his wife and two adult children were Christian caretakers of the family's Teréz körút home. They were witnesses for these inventory lists, their signatures at the bottom of the document certifying authenticity. The Dobó family, pretending to help, also offered to hide some of their belongings.

Caretakers were the administrators, managers, and guardians for the large Budapest apartments. It was a respectable and well-paid position. Caretakers lived in an apartment on the ground floor and monitored the traffic in and out of the buildings.

During the war, the Nazis used caretakers extensively as informants, and the Dobó family were suspected as being complicit. My family did not trust the Dobós. They believed they were spying on them, reporting their comings and goings to the police. In order to pacify the Dobós, Gábor wrote that István (Margit's brother) arranged for the Dobó's daughter to become caretaker of an apartment building at Éva utca, an investment property. The Dobó's son demanded the position of commander of the Teréz körút house. Through duplicitous means, the son compelled the family to rent some of the apartments to Christian families and other outsiders. A public institute in the neighborhood commandeered two of Ignácz's rooms. That is why Teréz körút could not be a yellow star house and the family was forced to move.

Most of the family's possessions, which Mrs. Dobó was supposed to keep safely hidden, disappeared. Gábor wrote that the family assumed the Dobó family had profited handsomely from the losses of the Misner/Politzer/Ambrus/Virány families.

On June 23rd, a wagon arranged for the move arrived at their Teréz körút home to transport their belongings to Személynök utca No.19 (today, Balassi Bálint utca 19), only a twenty-minute walk away, but a dark new world of deprivation, degradation, vulnerability, and indignity. Arrow Cross henchmen often raided the yellow star houses, terrorized the residents, and stole what little belongings they still had. István, Margit's brother, chose to go into hiding with a friend rather than move to the yellow star house.

In August 1944, after several weeks in the yellow star house, Margit, Bözsi, and Lili's family were visited by the Society of Christian Jews in Hungary. Bözsi had already converted to Catholicism in 1938. They convinced Margit and Lili's family to convert to Catholicism. It is unlikely they did this willingly, or for any other reason than to protect themselves.

As it turned out, conversion offered little protection. It is well known that the Catholic church's reaction to Jewish suffering under the Nazis was at best indifferent – at worst cruelly unsympathetic. Hungarian church leaders ignored requests from some of the bishops to rouse public opinion against the injustices committed against Jews. They supported the first two anti-Jewish laws. They objected to the third because it affected many of their parishioners – converted Jews and Christians who married Jews – and they wanted to retain the size of their congregations. Because of this, they pressured the Justice department to allow exemptions. That is why Ignácz could write his letter requesting exemption.

While Hungarian Christian church leaders were unsympathetic, there were many heroic priests and nuns who risked their lives to save Jews. One of those was Father József Jánosi, who helped found the Society of Christian Jews of Hungary to actively provide protection, aid, and comfort to its members. If Margit had mixed feelings about the conversion, the Society offered hope for protection during those ominous days. Once the Arrow Cross took over, all hope disappeared, and the Society was disbanded.

On October 15, 1944, the Germans toppled the Horthy government and replaced it with the murderous Arrow Cross party. It was rumored that even the Nazis were surprised at the brutality of the Hungarian Arrow

Cross. Jews, including those who had converted, were directed to move to the newly formed ghetto.

On October 20th, István, Margit's brother, came to the yellow star house to visit his family. A new decree extended the ages of men required to serve in forced labor units from 16 to 60. Knowing this, the caretaker of the house would not let István leave. The Arrow Cross was to round up more men the following morning. Although István was 66, older than the requirement, the caretaker turned him over to the Arrow Cross henchmen. Gábor's father, Alfréd, and uncle, caught in the same sweep, saw István at the sports field in Zuglo. Somehow, they were able to escape and upon their return reported this back to Margit and her family.

After several more days, the family still had not heard from István. In his book, Gábor described how "Margit tried to find her closest relatives, not sparing money and energy." She gave 10,000 pengo (the equivalent of $335,000 today) to two German Nazi soldiers in her desperation to find and bring home her brother. They discovered that shortly after being at Zuglo, István was driven by foot along with many elderly Jewish men to the village of Csomád. (see **Csomád on page 203**).

István Misner, circa 1910.

Eighteen months later, after the war had ended, my father identified István's body in the mass grave at Csomád. In his book, Gábor recounted how the socks and suspenders that István had worn for winter protection, were recognized as products of Gábor's uncle's textile factory, enabling identification of the body. Margit paid dearly to have his body moved to the family tomb.

Hiding Places

The yellow star houses were not safe, especially when deportations resumed at the end of August 1944. Beginning in July 1944, the Swedish Foreign Ministry (Raoul Wallenberg), the Swiss Consul (Carl Lutz), and Portuguese and Spanish legations issued international identity papers to protect Jews from deportation. Together with the Red Cross they also created "protected" houses to shelter them. These safe houses, 120 across Budapest, took in thousands of Jews. At the end of November, Jews were being forced into the ghetto and the deportations were accelerated. Margit and her family members had to go into hiding, either to protected houses or to Christian friends. There were relatively few Christians who had the courage and compassion to help.

The remaining members of the family had to split up. Except for Ignácz, Alfréd, and Gábor, the men of the family were gone. István was taken to Csomád, Bözsi's husband, Sándor, was arrested (his story told in **Chapter 14**), and my father had been moved to a forced labor camp in the Bükk mountains in Slovakia (his story told in **Chapter 15**). The Arrow Cross left only the elderly, children, and women to fend for themselves. Margit took charge once again, trying to save her family.

Using her web of relatives, friends, and servants, Margit tried to make sure that her family was safe, their material needs met. She paid servants to brave the treacherous streets, buy goods on the black market and deliver them to everyone's hiding places. She even tried to maintain celebrations, sending family members gifts on their birthdays, and pastries, chocolates or candies for the holidays.

My mother, Clara, engaged to my father at the time, was one of the Christians who delivered messages to various family members. She also brought Bözsi, my grandmother, from the yellow star house to the factory complex where she was hiding others (her story is also told in **Chapter 15**). At great risk to herself, she also helped Lili, Alfréd and Gábor escape from the ghetto and took them to another hiding place.

It was Margit who had secured a room for her father, Ignácz, in a nursing home on Géllert Hill. She could not know that within two months he would starve to death in a ghetto hospital.

With each move, their living conditions deteriorated. Gábor described the protected house (most likely under Swiss protection), where he and his parents moved, as an apartment with three rooms and a hall. Forty people lived there, and the congestion made life difficult if not unbearable. They put three mattresses and a table in the hall, and that is where they stayed for three weeks. They almost never went out. It was too dangerous.

One day, Lili left to visit Margit, who had moved to a protected house nearby. That day, as Gábor recounted, the Arrow Cross raided the house. Lili was chased by a thug who screamed, "I will shoot you! I will shoot you!" Somehow, she managed to escape.

Margit at age 68 had to move again. One of her Christian classmates took her in. After five days, that became too dangerous. Neighbors were monitoring neighbors. One account described how the janitor came to register the amount of hot water used. Few could be trusted, given the penalties faced by those harboring fugitives and the rewards offered to informants. Bubi, the son of Margit's closest friend (who had died the year before of colon cancer), helped to take Margit to another Christian friend's house in the Rózsadomb section of the Buda Hills.

Margit's sister, Gizella, and Gizella's husband, Frigyes Tibold, were last seen in a protected house in December. They were having difficulty moving due to health issues and were hopeful that they would continue to be safe by staying put. But the Arrow Cross raided the house and took everyone away. Someone saw Frigyes carrying a pack at the Nyugati-railway station, the Budapest station close to their Teréz körút home.

I wondered if they were taken to Auschwitz. I wrote to the Arolsen Archives, the Holocaust Survivors Database, Yad Vashem and Auschwitz. Nothing came back. We will never know if Gizella and Frigyes died in one of the death marches to the Austrian border, or were herded to the banks of the Danube, made to strip naked, and shot into the freezing water. Throughout my search, I often thought about the despair Margit faced. No bodies were found. There could be no burials.

Gizella and Frigyes Tibold, circa 1905.

The Siege of Budapest

With the arrival of Russian troops on Christmas 1944, the six-week siege of Budapest began. It was one of the bloodiest sieges of World War II. Both Hitler and Stalin demanded victory at all costs, attesting to Budapest's strategic importance.

Fighting was particularly intense in the Buda Hills where Margit was hiding. The hilly terrain allowed the Germans to position artillery fortifications above the Soviet attackers. Fierce fighting broke out, not only around

Castle Hill and the Royal Palace, but also in the less populated areas where affluent Hungarians, such as the Politzer family and friends, owned villas.

I had assumed that Margit was hidden by her close friend's daughter-in-law, Eva, who lived in the Rózsadomb section of the Buda Hills. Later I found out this was not true, though she did visit Eva during the siege.

Seventy years later, my sister Kathy questioned Eva and learned more about their story. Eva and Margit were in the living room at Eva's parents' house. They heard a loud unfamiliar sound, somewhat like an organ. It was a Russian plane flying very low with small caliber artillery shooting straight into the house. They ran down to the bunker. But there was too much heat. The house was on fire. They ran out of the house, dodging bullets, and dove into the bushes for cover. Learning this, I ached for Margit - 68 years old, weak from hunger and terrified, running for her life in the frigid winter air.

When Eva told this story to my sister, Eva was 98 years old. Her mind was sharp, but her health was failing. My sister did not ask for more details. I wished for more. How had they survived in the woods? How did they get to safety? Where did she live after her house burned? Did she know who hid Margit? How did Margit come to visit her? How did they persevere under such extreme conditions? I can only assume the story had shocked my sister into silence.

Photo of the apartment building on Margit körút after the bombing that killed Zoltán Ambrus, January 1945. Fortepan / Military Museum of Southern New England.

Soviet troops in Budapest. Csepel,
II. Rákóczi Ferenc street. 1945.
Fortepan / Fortepan.

Russian soldiers standing close to the
destroyed. Elizabeth bridge.
Fortepan / Fortepan.

During the siege, shelling and the bombing were constant. The streets were perilous. Food and water were scarce. Thousands of people prowled the streets after dark, foraging for scraps of food. They carved up frozen horses for meat and melted snow for water. With no electricity, no plumbing, no heat, unsanitary and crowded conditions, and lice infestations, there was fear of a typhus epidemic.

The siege was still underway, when on January 23, 1945, Margit's hiding place in Rózsadomb was bombed. Gábor wrote that Margit planned to move in with Bözsi's brother-in-law, Zoltán Ambrus, who was hidden by his Christian wife. Fortunately, her plans were diverted. On her way, she ran into one of Gábor's uncles who wanted to check out their summer villa in Buda. She briefly stayed with him, rather than making the treacherous journey to Pest. Zoltán died that day when his house was bombed. The valuable objects Zoltán had hidden for my father's and Gábor's family were destroyed.

Margit moved with Gábor's uncle to another house in Buda where Gábor's aunt was hiding. I read that civilians went to the cellars "like rats" and did not emerge until the German/ Hungarian surrender on February 13th. But it seemed that Margit moved around, possibly out of necessity but perhaps to safeguard her family and friends.

Returning Home

More violence followed the German/Hungarian surrender. In Buda alone, an estimated two thousand wounded were burned or suffocated in fires that broke out in the catacombs under the Royal Palace. Budapest lay in ruins. Thousands of structures, including the Parliament building, were destroyed or damaged. All five of the city's bridges were blown up by the retreating German army and collapsed into the Danube. Almost 40,000 Hungarian civilians, half of them Jewish, died in the carnage. An unknown number died of starvation and disease. Mass rapes of women between the ages of 10 and 80 were common. In Budapest alone an estimated 50,000 women were said to have been raped by Romanian and Red Army soldiers. What unimaginable horrors did Margit experience?

It would be another month until Margit returned to Pest and her beloved home on Teréz körút, where the building lay in shambles, an entire side struck by a bomb. Rooms were gutted and filled with debris. There was no plumbing nor electricity.

Gábor recounted in his book that he was having dinner with his parents in the kitchen of their apartment, lit only by candlelight. Later that evening an old acquaintance emerged. She said she brought a guest. When they realized Margit had returned, they jumped up for joy.

How Margit returned is a "heroic act," as Gábor described. She walked. It is only six or so miles. But she had to cross hills, bomb craters, trenches, and roads strewn with rubble, wreckage, and the dead bodies of people and animals. On her journey, she had missed the last boat that crossed the Danube at Batthyány Square and thus had to walk across the recently built temporary bridge. She stopped at the apartment of someone named Gida. We don't know if Gida was a friend or a previous servant. Perhaps still fearing for her own life, rather than giving Margit sanctuary, Gida escorted Margit home. Margit arrived exhausted from her walk and nine months of dodging danger.

Families returning home after Germany surrenders, February 1945. Fortepan / Fortepan.

The destroyed Chain Bridge, 1945. Fortepan / Military Museum of Southern New England.

Crossing the Danube in boats. Fortepan / Rózsa László.

We will never know the details of where, what, and how Margit survived. Once home, her priority was to find her family. It would be several months before Margit could learn their various fates. She lost her father, her brother and sister, her brother-in-law, her son-in-law, and her son-in-law's brother. Of her relatives on the Politzer side, at least twenty-five aunts, uncles, cousins, nieces and nephews were killed. There were another forty Politzers for whom we don't have dates of death. The fates of her other relatives – Misners, Morgensterns, Markbreits, Háys, Ösztreichers – mostly remain a mystery.

Margit struggled to find a final resting place for those who had perished. She had converted to Christianity when she moved to the yellow star house, but her Jewish faith remained strong. She would honor their memory by adhering to Jewish tradition as best she could. She paid dearly to bring her loved ones to the family tomb in the Jewish cemetery on Kozma Street.

We don't know when and how Margit learned of her father's (Ignácz) death. We found documents in the box (rescued from my parents' home) in which she repeatedly requested to have his body exhumed so that it could be moved to the family tomb. Her requests were denied. Only his name is inscribed on the tombstone.

Despite the "conversion" to Catholicism, Margit continued to practice Judaism. In the box were two tickets dated 1949 for the high holidays at the Dohány Synagogue, one for Margit and the other for Ignácz. It is a mystery why five years after his death, Margit still had a ticket for Ignácz. She may have used the ticket for a male friend or cousin.

A New Normal

In April 1945, my parents, newly married, returned to Budapest from Szeged, where they were in medical school (see **Chapter 15**). The marriage came as a shock to my father's mother, Bözsi. My mother was Catholic of modest means. An outsider. Not my Grandmother Bözsi's idea of an appropriate match for her son - a wealthy Jewish bride with social status.

Later, I learned that according to Bözsi, my father's intended was supposed to be one of her friend's daughters. Margit, on the other hand, accepted my mother with grace and love and encouraged Bözsi to do the same.

Dohány-utcai templomi

imaszék-igazolvány
másodlat

Dr.Misner Ignác   ur

....*részére.*

Férfi *osztály* 52   *pad* 1   *ülés.*

FIGYELMEZTETÉS! Ez az igazolvány jól meg-
őrzendő, mert a főünnepekre szóló belépőjegy csak
ennek előmutatása ellenében adatik ki.

Dohány-utcai templomi

imaszék-igazolvány
másodlat

Dr.Politzer Gyuláné urnő

....*részére.*

Női *osztály* 50   *pad* 2   *ülés.*

FIGYELMEZTETÉS! Ez az igazolvány jól meg-
őrzendő, mert a főünnepekre szóló belépőjegy csak
ennek előmutatása ellenében adatik ki.

PESTI IZRAELITA HITKÖZSÉG

VII., SIP-UTCA 12.

442/10.......... *iktatószám.*

Imaszék-igazolvány.
másodlat

A pesti izr. hitközség előljárósága igazolja, hogy a hitközség **Dohány-utcai**
jobboldalon
templomának **női** *osztályán és pedig a*...*levő*

50 / Ötven /.....................*pad* 2 / Kettő /...............*ülésszámu*

imaszék **használati joga,** *a templomi imaszékek nyilvántartó törzskönyvének* 433

lapján az 19.....*évi*...............*hó*.....*napján fenti iktatószám alatt történt hivatalos*

bejegyzésnek megfelelően, ezidőszerint.....Dr.Politzer Gyuláné

....*illeti meg.*

Budapesten, 19 49 *évi* augusztus *hó* 24 *napján.*

Az előljáróság megbizásából:

főtanácsos.

High holiday tickets for the Dohány Synagogue, 1949.

Margit bought them wedding bands. Although the rings were simple gold bands, it was an extravagant gesture, given the scarcity of food, run-away inflation, and challenging living conditions. Margit understood what the generosity of spirit embodied in this gesture would mean to this young couple.

Margit had little time to mourn. She had to take stock of family assets that could be recovered. Her brother, István, who had taken care of family matters, was dead. Her son-in-law, Sándor Ambrus, my grandfather, was dead. She could not depend on her other son-in-law, Alfréd, Gábor's father, to support the family, especially since his factory had been expropriated and later closed. My father was a young medical student, concentrating on his studies. As matriarch of the family, she needed to find a way for the family to survive. Post-war Hungary experienced the worst hyperinflation ever recorded. In July 1946, Hungarian prices more than tripled each day. Margit sold family properties at heartbreaking prices.

Aside from his law practice, Margit's brother, István, had been an active real estate developer through his company Sunshine Builders. Several family members were stockholders, including Margit. András and I tracked down their latest development, a four-story apartment house at Éva utca 15 (currently Asbóth utca), completed in 1940/1941.

In January 1946, Margit, acting as guardian delegated by the chancery on behalf of István, called an emergency meeting. The first order of business was to force the resignation of Mrs. István Dobó, who had become the acting caretaker of the Teréz körút house after her son left and her husband died.

Teréz körút 45 had been Margit's beacon of hope throughout the war years – if she could get her family back home, they would be safe. But that was not to be. In addition to the tragic loss of close family, her possessions, her art collection, and her homes were gone. Teréz körút was barely livable.

Hungary was the slowest among the European countries to rebuild. Even after several years, much rubble remained to be cleared. According to my mother, my father's favorite uncle, Imre Kovács, was an architect helping to rebuild the city. He died in 1951, when loose bricks from an apartment building crushed him. His will, leaving everything to my father, was in the box that was sent to me. Later, I learned that his brother, my father's other favorite uncle, had been murdered in Auschwitz.

John Lukacs in his book, *Budapest 1900*, described those years:

> *An atmosphere of fearsome decay stood silent in Budapest streets, hemmed in by the pockmarked walls of apartment houses built in another time, even dingier and more broken down. The once fine vista of palatial buildings and hotels along the Danube quays was gone. The line of buildings was broken by rubble-strewn lots. The sunlit face of the self-confident young matron that Budapest had once been was now disfigured by toothless gaps.*

Imre Kovács, my father's favorite uncle, circa 1930.

The Communist Era

After the defeat of the Germans, the allies (United States, Britain, France, and the Soviet Union) established the Allied Control Commission (ACC) to control the defeated countries (Germany, Italy and Japan). Under the ACC, Hungary rebuilt a democracy which lasted for two years. Although the United States and Britain participated in the ACC, they did not challenge the Soviet Union's encroachment on the Eastern Bloc countries and their authoritarian control.

After Stalin seized Poland, Czechoslovakia, and Romania (1946-1948), he turned his attention to Hungary. The Soviets established a brutal secret police unit, the ÁVO (Államvedelmi Osztály). Over 200,000 Hungarian citizens, including political leaders, were imprisoned, conscripted into forced labor, or relocated. Political opponents were tried in "show trials" and executed. By 1948, the Soviets had replaced the Hungarian democracy with a repressive communist regime. It was a period of aggressive nationalization of factories, banks, and businesses, the collectivization of agriculture, and harassment and intimidation by secret police.

In Margit's Teréz körút home, the apartments were divided into smaller ones accommodating several families. Margit became a tenant in her home, allowed to rent only two rooms. Her numerous requests to the Ministry of Interior for more rooms were denied. Even the name of her street no longer existed. Teréz körút was renamed Lenin körút.

In the summer of 1951, 15,000 citizens were expatriated from their apartments in Budapest with 24 hours to pack their lifetime belongings. The Communist regime worked to confiscate apartments and valuables from the rich, "bourgeois" capitalists, who were stigmatized as "enemies of the people." They were assigned to new residences in rural, agricultural villages. Kuláks (prosperous peasants who were also considered class enemies) were forced to house the families. Local citizens were forbidden to talk with the "enemies of the people." As the Nazis had dehumanized the Jews, the Soviets dehumanized capitalists with a modicum of wealth (including successful Jews), calling them "snakes" or "vermin." They were kept under constant police surveillance, implemented through periodic reporting to the local government office and random visits by police officers to the assigned homes, often in the middle of the night.

That same summer, Margit and Bözsi were expelled from their home and assigned to live with a family in Nagyréde, 50 miles northeast of Budapest. Margit, 75 at the time, was not in good health, and wrote that Bözsi was also sick and very depressed. Yet they were required to work. What kind of work, Bözsi never revealed, nor did she speak about that time.

Margit appealed to the minister of the interior. She wrote that although she had inherited three properties (her home at Teréz körút, her villa at Sváb Hill, and a third building on Liszt Ferencz square), the inheritance taxes and repairs depleted all her resources. She had to sell the property on Liszt Ferencz square to pay the inheritance tax. She had to sell her personal possessions and take out a roof loan in order to make Teréz körút livable.

In spite of these hardships, she helped others. She gave up her furniture, offered free rent, and paid taxes for a poor tenant who had nothing.

She continued the appeal to the interior minister, explaining the deaths of family members and the difficulties she'd endured. She also stated:

> *(I write) in the hope that Mr. Minister of Interior will establish that I was not a capitalist, nor was I exploiting anybody, but the opposite. My tragic inheritance only brought problems and poverty for me at my old age. My daughter's situation was even more serious than mine, since she lost her husband and her dependency on me made her depressed.*

The appeal was rejected. Was it because Margit's properties put her in the category of a rich, "bourgeois" capitalist, or because her grandson, my father, "defected"? My parents left Hungary in 1947 to complete their studies in the highly regarded medical school in Zurich. By 1951, when Margit wrote this letter, my parents had emigrated to the US. (see **Chapter 15**).

On March 29, 1952, Margit received a message from the Budapest District Court. On a small impersonal form sent to her in Nagyréde, she was informed that her Teréz körút home had been officially confiscated by the state. She received similar notices for the villa in Sváb Hill. She had paid the inheritance tax. She had paid for all the repairs. And after the payments bankrupted her, the state took her ownership rights. She was left with nothing. None of her numerous appeals altered the power of those small four-by-five-inch pieces of paper.

The document which informed Margit that her Teréz körút home was confiscated by the communist government. 1952.

Lili was occasionally allowed to visit her mother and sister, as somehow Lili and Alfréd avoided this fate and were able to remain in Budapest. Margit and Bözsi returned to Budapest in 1953, after Stalin's death and restrictions loosened. They were able to rent back their rooms on Teréz körút, even though they no longer owned their home.

With each year, the effort to extract Margit and Bözsi from Hungary intensified. Margit's cousin, Gizella, and husband Leó Müller, living in Paris, wrote letter upon letter to Hungarian authorities, requesting their emigration to France. Similarly, my parents, now in the US, spent considerable resources to explore every possible way for them to immigrate to the US. The 1956 revolution provided that opportunity. Unfortunately, Margit was 80 at that time and not in good health. Only Bözsi was able to leave.

As Margit approached her 80s, she had so little left. Having friends and relatives over for tea gave her joy. This simple meal was the best she could muster in her old age. She wanted to entertain in the style she was used to: a table set with beautiful linen, china, and silverware. However, the china and silverware had been confiscated by the Nazis. Some linens given to her by her mother, Jozefa, were all that remained. When, in 1958, these were stolen by a dry cleaner, it felt like the last injustice. Margit wrote a letter of complaint to a Budapest newspaper, in the hopes of having it published. It never was.

> *I am an 82-year-old widow, my vision and my hearing have both been deteriorating. Whatever little joy left in my life is that using my savings I invite my closest relatives for an afternoon tea 2-3 times a year. It was about time, again, to gather the family at the home of the oldest member that is myself. Therefore, I took my cherished tablecloths to the Patyolat (dry cleaning) at Buday László street to have them washed. I had been given these by my beloved mother for my dowry and I hardly used them. During the busy days before the holidays the package was delivered long after the deadline... Instead of the linen-damask tablecloths they were trying to give me two small colorful cotton tablecloths that I obviously refused to accept... These tablecloths are irreplaceable: such material has hardly even been imported since the Liberation and I have not been able to afford even the table ware from Bizományi Áruház (second-hand chain stores before 1990). Despite my old age, I still give language courses at Tanimpex company at 7 in the morning twice a week, to supplement my pension and improve my financial situation...*

Margit had a weak heart. Her health started to deteriorate. In letters found in the box, she wrote to friends and family members that she was always tired and often had to lie down. Reading and writing letters (she wrote extensively) made her tired. Although her legs were swollen and it was difficult to walk, she tried to visit with friends every day, either inviting them to her home or meeting them at Hotel Béke (The Britannia renamed) next door. In a letter to Marianne O, her best friend's daughter, she thanked her for a check, saying, "...although with my pension I do not have to pay for the hospital or medication, but one needs to give so much in tips that amounts to a high salary." Free health care under communism was not very free.

Mostly Margit wrote that she wanted to travel to Vienna to meet Bözsi. In a letter to her cousin Richard, she wrote "I am so afraid that I will turn in the application again in vain, so far I have always been rejected. But I am trying anyways. I would like to see Bözsi once more in this life. This one hope keeps me alive that this visit might once materialize."

Bözsi was able to visit Budapest in the fall of 1961. Margit died February 7, 1962. The cause of death was heart failure.

I wish, knowing what I know now, that I could have heard directly from Bözsi about her amazing mother, my great-grandmother.

Lili, Margit, and Bözsi in Budapest in 1961, the last time they were together.

LEARNING MORE

Antisemitic Violence in the Aftermath of World War I

White Terror Units Next to Margit's Home

In World War I, many young Jewish men fought valiantly and received medals of distinction. It was thought that after the war, there would be no more anti-Semitic agitation. Jews would claim full equality. But this was not to be.

With the defeat in World War I, Hungary was thrown into chaos. A devastating outbreak of Spanish flu, a prolonged fuel shortage, and the fear of territorial disintegration destabilized the newly formed Hungarian People's Republic. In March 1919, Béla Kun seized control and declared Hungary a Soviet Republic. The communist government lasted only 133 days, leaving a legacy of an ill-fated war with Romania and a campaign known as the "Red Terror." However, repercussions from secret tribunals, secret police, and revolutionary courts used to murder and terrorize the population lasted far longer than the government's 133 days. Kun and many of his top-ranking officials were Jewish. After Kun's government fell, a new regime under the leadership of Miklós Horthy became the first post-World War I nationalist dictatorship in Europe. It began a ruthless period of retribution called the "White Terror."

For eighteen months (1919-1920), right wing army officers, civic guards, and local police, joined paramilitary units called the White Guard, and carried out unimaginable atrocities against any suspected communists, including Jews, in the name of nationalism. Pál Prónay, one of the most sadistic paramilitary commanders, established his unit in the Hotel Britannia, next door to Margit's Teréz körút home.

The building that housed the Hotel Britannia was meant to be a mansion. In 1913, Henrik Fábri purchased the mansion and the apartment building behind it. He combined them and built an exclusive first-class hotel. No expense was spared. The hotel was outfitted with extraordinary modern conveniences: running hot and cold water in each room, steam and water-based central heating, hotel laundry, central vacuum cleaner, and a room service system operating with light indicators. The hall was decorated with wood paneling and bronze chandeliers. The restaurant was covered by a glass roof brilliantly illuminated night and day. The basement could house 30 cars.

HOTEL-GARAGE BRITANNIA, BUDAPEST

Basement of the Hotel Britannia before it became a torture chamber during the White Terror, 1919-1920. / A képeslap a szerencsi Zempléni Múzeum gyűjteményéből származik.

The hotel's illustrious guest list included landowners from the countryside, professionals, and merchants, along with foreign factory owners. It was a popular place until Prónay's savage paramilitary unit took it over. The basement was turned into a torture chamber.

In their bestial hatred they made no distinction between communists, Soviet-sympathizers, socialists, leftist intellectuals, and Jews. Women were violated and had their breasts cut off. Men were broken on the rack and beaten to obtain "voluntary confessions." Men, women, and children were brutally maimed. The savagery of the White Terror was not contained within the Hotel Britannia. Other commanders committed similar brutalities throughout the city and the country. But Prónay was known for his fanaticism and cruelty. An estimated 5,000 people were tortured and killed and over 75,000 imprisoned.

Hungary's Numerus Clausus of 1920

The Numerus Clausus Act, passed in September 1920, was the first anti-Semitic law of the post-World War I era in Europe. It signaled the start of a new period for Hungarian Jews, denying them the equality they had won in 1895. It reduced Jewish admissions into universities. With severe limits on women's admissions, it secured the male, Christian, nationalist, conservative predominance of the Magyar nobility.

With its passing, thousands of Jewish students left Hungary to finish their studies abroad. Such was the fate for scientist Leo Szilard, known for his work on the nuclear chain reaction. Szilard was one of the greatest minds in physics, yet he was denied entry into a Hungarian university and continued his studies in Berlin. Henrik Marczali, Ignácz Misner's cousin who had written a widely acclaimed history of Hungary within the Habsburg Empire, was suddenly dismissed from his university post in Budapest and never employed again. The restrictions were eased but not repealed in 1928.

Recovery After World War I

Horthy, regent and leader of Hungary, appointed Count István Bethlen prime minister in 1921 (until 1931). Bethlen, a shrewd statesman, was able to bring order to the economy. Hungarian Jews hoped that the violence of the White Terror had been an anomaly and that their relations with non-Jewish Hungarian society could be restored. They continued to place a strong emphasis on the Hungarian aspects of their identity hoping this would help revive the prewar balance. John Lukacs, in *Budapest 1900*, best described the interwar years:

> *Hungary and Hungarians ... have an instinctive genius for recovery after their worst disasters. A semblance of peace began to spread over the capital and the country.... People in Budapest breathed freer. The air became lighter. Here and there the city began to sparkle anew...Financial stability and a measure of industrial prosperity returned. The high standards of education and publishing climbed to their earlier prewar standards, even surpassing them in some instances. The years 1921 to 1935 could be called the Silver Age of modern Hungarian letters.*

The cafés once again filled with writers, poets, journalists, actors, artists, and other intellectuals. Once more, theaters, concerts, operas, and cinemas drew large audiences. Women dressed in the latest fashions purchased from elegant shops. Tourists began to flood into the city enchanted by its beauty and sophistication. H.L Mencken (1880-1956), an American journalist, essayist and cultural critic wrote to his wife in 1930:

> *It (Budapest) is by far the most beautiful that I have ever seen. I came expecting to see a somewhat dingy copy of Vienna, but it makes Vienna look like a village. There is something thoroughly royal about it... The Danube is under my window, and across the river, on a range of hills, lies a long series of truly superb palaces.*

Csomád

Csomád is a small village 20 miles northeast of Budapest. It was the site of one of the Jewish labor camps.

In 1945-1946, the Hungarian Jewish relief organization, National Committee for Attending Deportees (DEGOB) recorded personal stories of Hungarian Holocaust survivors. Researching Csomád on their website, I found several horrific stories. One such story recounted:

> We were escorted by the Arrow Cross men, who behaved more brutally than the SS. When we arrived in Csomád 4 days later we had already had casualties, as the Arrow Cross men shot dead a few men. Before our departure they had tortured us. We were tired, hungry, and psychically tormented.

Their accommodations were a brick factory with little protection from the elements. They were forced to dig deep trenches to stave off Soviet tanks and subjected to the whims of cruel guards.

Ernő Szép, a well-known Hungarian poet and novelist, wrote about his experience at Csomád in his book, *The Smell of Humans: A Memoir of the Holocaust in Hungary*. I wondered if he met István. Having become very ill, Ernő was given permission to stay back in a make-shift infirmary. A fellow prisoner came to the infirmary, starving and visibly worse off than Ernő. When Ernő generously gave him a left-over morsel of stale bread, he described ironically how this mate, so appreciative, owned 10,000 acres of farmland. Ernő found out the next day that this mate was forced to dig his own grave. I wonder if this could have been my great uncle István. I imagine many others who have read his book might wonder about the experience of a loved one during that dreadful period.

FAMILY TREE

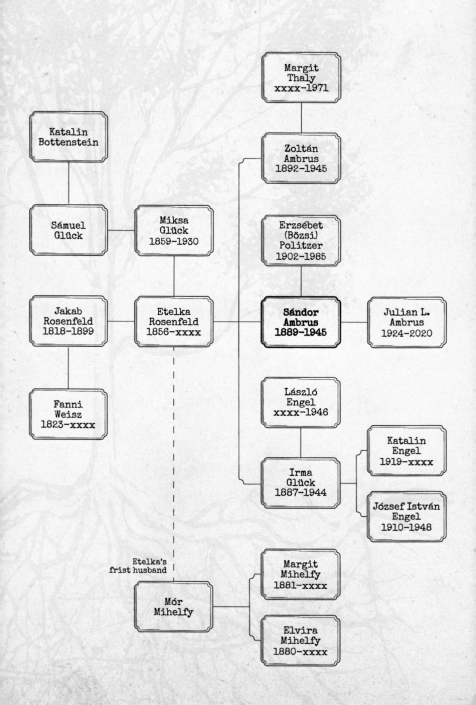

Chapter 14

Sándor Ambrus

Sándor Ambrus (1889-1945) was my grandfather. My father and my mother revealed little about his life and nothing about his death. Even my grandmother, Bözsi, who came to live with us, rarely spoke about her husband, Sándor. As I searched for my father's family, I learned more about my remarkable grandfather, about his life and death. That story is told here.

The Man with the Mustache

A large oil painting of my grandfather hung in my parent's dining room. It meant little to me growing up in our house in Buffalo, an unfamiliar face of a man with a mustache, no more interesting than other paintings brought from Hungary. I knew this man was my father's father, my grandmother's husband. But they rarely spoke of him or answered questions about him. I stopped asking.

Painting of my grandfather, Sándor Ambrus, that hung in my parents' dining room.

But sometimes, perhaps hoping to appease my persistent curiosity, my grandmother, Bözsi, who had come to live with us in 1956, would reveal little nuggets. On those few occasions, she would lift her head gazing into some unknown distance. A veil of sadness and longing would come over her when she spoke.

I learned that my grandfather, Sándor, had been a prominent lawyer and a senior executive in a large bank. She told me he was tall and handsome. Very honest. And that the Nazis took him as a political prisoner because he was a leading citizen in the community. She never hinted that it was because he was Jewish. He didn't try to avoid the call from the Nazis. He thought turning himself in would protect his family. She told me this when I knew nothing of my Jewish heritage. I didn't question why the family needed protection.

In 2005, my nephew, Alexander, asked my father for help with his 7th grade class project. He needed to write an essay about an ancestor. My father wrote: "Your great-grandfather, whom you were named after, (Sándor is Hungarian for Alexander) grew up on the family farm and in high school as well as at the university, was a champion high jumper and tennis player. He was a great horseman. He was a talented poet and had a great sense of humor." He never mentioned that Sándor was Jewish.

My father, proud of Sándor's heroism in World War I, added more to the story, writing that Sándor was a first lieutenant and fought on the Russian front. As with most cavalry forces, he lost his unit and his horses to artillery fire. He was transferred to Albania to be the Judge Advocate General. On his return to Vienna, his ship was torpedoed, and yet he survived this and many other harrowing ordeals.

Sámuel Glück

When I began to explore my family history, I was shocked to learn that my grandfather, known to me as Sándor Ambrus, was born Sámuel Glück on August 23, 1889, in Sajószentpéter, Hungary (northeast of Budapest). He was named after his grandfather.

Sámuel was the second of three children born to Miksa Glück (1859 - 1930) and Etelka Rosenfeld (1861 - unknown date). It was a second marriage for both. Miksa was a widower. Etelka a divorcee. Divorce was extremely rare for religious Jews at that time and only possible in highly justified cases. András was able to locate the divorce papers. Etelka's divorce settlement had provided her and her two daughters a considerable sum. (see **Members of the Rosenfeld Family are Talented Writers on page 217**)

Sámuel and his younger brother Zoltán attended the State Main Scientific Secondary School in Debrecen from ages 10 through 17. Science schools placed a strong emphasis on modern languages, mathematics and science as opposed to the grammar schools which provided a liberal arts and classics (Latin and Greek) education. The academic standards were high. Sámuel excelled, receiving top marks.

Sámuel was president of the Literary Study Group. In 1907, the school dedicated a new flag. Sámuel's poem for the occasion won first prize. He was asked to give the speech at the flag-raising ceremony. Discovering his poem and speech, András commented, "They are remarkable, written in an ancient Hungarian language. Today most Hungarians would hardly understand it."

Hungary has a strong tradition of poetry. One of the most admired poets was Sándor Petőfi, whose patriotic poems inspired the revolution of 1848. Sámuel greatly admired Petőfi. With the flag as its symbol, his speech had a similar patriotic fervor. Loyalty to school and country, and gratitude for education were its themes. Mature beyond his 17 years, he spoke about the trinity of religion, homeland, and science, and how education was the path to "strength, knowledge and power."

Although he hadn't taken Latin in school, Sámuel passed the Latin exam, required for admittance into law school. He enrolled at the Royal Hungarian University of Pest, graduating in 1912.

Embroidered on the back of Sándor's school flag are the words, "Education is strength and power".

How did Sámuel Glück become Sándor Ambrus? He changed his name from Sámuel to Sándor in his second or third year at university. Four years later, Sándor and his younger brother Zoltán changed their surname to Ambrus. This pronouncement appeared in the Budapesti Hirlap (a national daily newspaper) on April 28, 1912.

What possesses a young man at the age of 23 to change his name? I had read how Hungary encouraged Jews to change their names to Hungarian names in an effort to tip the demographic balance between nationalities within the Austro-Hungarian empire. Did my grandfather change his name solely out of loyalty to his country? Or did he want to change his identity? Why did he choose Ambrus? It was not a common surname. Did he choose it because it was a less Jewish sounding name that would allow him to navigate the world more easily, especially a career in law? Or did he choose it in deference to Zoltán Ambrus (1861-1932), the famous writer who was also from Debrecen?

Changing his name coincided with graduating from university and becoming a junior lawyer. In Hungary, lawyers apprenticed for two to three years before being accepted into the Bar. He passed the bar exam in January 1915. Then, with the call of World War I, he enlisted.

Challenging Circumstances

We don't know when Sándor returned from World War I and started his law practice. We only know that in June 1919, after the end of World War I, Sándor was drafted into the Red Army. Hungarian communists under the leadership of Béla Kun had seized control of the government in a campaign known as "Red Terror" and instituted the Hungarian Soviet Republic (see **Chapter 13**). Sándor served as a junior officer for less than two months. The Hungarian Soviet Republic and its Red Army collapsed on August 1, 1919, when Horthy overthrew Béla Kun and his government. Horthy's new government screened all lawyers in a verification process for readmission into the bar. In 1920, the Military Gazette determined that Sándor had an exemplary record as a former first lieutenant and military judge. Although he served as a Red soldier, he did not commit any crimes.

From the time Sándor entered law school until 1920, Hungary had experienced four different political systems, including a communist regime that did not recognize the legal profession. When Horthy's government came to power, Sándor received approval (or re-approval) into the bar on December 1919. Finally, he was able to start his practice.

Sándor married Bözsi, my grandmother, on January 14th, 1923, when he was 33 years old. My father, their only child, was born 22 months later, on November 29, 1924.

Sándor Ambrus' acceptance into
the Budapest Bar Association, 1919.

Sándor took over as the general counsel for Kőbánya Savings Bank, a position which his deceased father-in-law, Gyula Politzer, had held. His private law offices were on the second floor of the Teréz körút house, down the hall from their living quarters. Every day he returned from the bank to eat lunch at home at 3:00 PM (the main meal) and to read his daily newspapers. Then he worked in his private office until 8 PM. His corporate clients came from all over the world – but mostly from Germany, Austria, and England.

On July 24, 1930, Sándor survived an assassination attempt. The assassin barged into his Teréz körút office and fired a shot from a Browning revolver. The assassin, Béla Türichter, had been a wealthy slipper maker who came back from the war disabled and psychotic. Sándor had ended a call with Türichter's lawyer to negotiate a settlement on two defaulted loans with the bank. A maid, hearing the shots, called the police who took Türichter away. Sándor was unharmed. The incident, however, received extensive coverage in the newspapers.

Newspaper headlines of the attempted assassination of Sándor, 1930.

Such bizarre acts of aggression were not foreign to Sándor. Béla Fábián (1889-1967) was one of his closest friends. Béla was the president of the Hungarian National Democratic party and a member of the Hungarian parliament for 17 years. He was the major opposition to the Horthy government's pro-Nazi faction. He frequently got into trouble, and Sándor would bail him out. My father said that such trouble often involved duels, although illegal. Both Béla and Sándor were excellent swordsmen. Sándor took lessons from Mr. Sztankay, a national champion. I was skeptical until I read that one Hungarian newspaper reported at least 40 duels were scheduled in one week alone during November 1927 between Jewish students and anti-Semites.

Eleven years later, with the enactment of the anti-Jewish Laws, antisemitism would be officially sanctioned. The first Jewish Law, passed in May 1938, limited the ratio of Jewish lawyers to twenty percent. Jewish was defined on religious grounds. In May 1939, the second Jewish law defined Jews on racial grounds – you were considered Jewish if just one grandparent was Jewish, regardless of what religion you practiced – and restricted their number to six percent of the professions.

Sándor faced immense pressure maintaining his career both at the bank and with his private law practice. In July 1938, completing his annual registration form for the Bar Association, he wrote "Israelite" in response to the question of religion. Later that year, on December 18, 1938, Sándor and

Bözsi converted to Catholicism. When Sándor renewed his registration in October 1939, he declared his religion Roman Catholic, but at the bottom had to state, "I declare that I am to be regarded as being Jewish."

Professionally, the conversion would have been important to maintain his network of friends and colleagues. He took clients to extravagant dinners, to the opera (his favorite composer was Wagner), and to the theater. He played tennis with people like Count Imre Zichy (1908-1999), a three-time winner of the Hungarian National Tennis Championships in doubles. He socialized with the elite, frequenting their weekend hunting parties, balls, and bridge parties.

Even with the increasing pressures of the Jewish laws, Sándor tried to maintain a semblance of normalcy. In his book, Gábor described those normal activities: a tennis match on Margaret Island (May 30, 1943); dinner and theater for Margit's birthday (October 18, 1943); a pig roast hosted by Bözsi's former dance teacher (December 1944); the purchase of an elegant ball gown for the premiere of the Richard Strauss opera "Der Rosenkavalier" (January 1944).

My grandmother Bözsi and my grandfather Sándor, circa 1930.

Facing Evil

Despite the war moving towards Budapest, on Saturday, March 18, 1944, Sándor and Bözsi attended a ball at the mansion of the Ford company representative to Hungary. They made it home at early dawn without a problem. They had a relaxing breakfast. Margit's hairdresser set her hair, a weekly ritual. The cooks prepared lunch. They were finishing their dessert when the phone rang. My father's former tutor was calling to tell Sándor that the Germans had arrived. Adolf Eichmann and the Nazis were marching into the city. Gábor wrote in his book, "The Ambrus family hid a lot of stuff that day."

A month later, on April 24th, a messenger brought a note to Sándor that he was to report to the Gestapo prison in three days. Friends and family begged him not to go. He could get false papers and go into hiding. But he feared that doing so would endanger his family. On April 27th he was escorted to the Jewish Theological Seminary on Rökk Szilárd utca, which had been turned into an auxiliary detention house.

On June 26th, Sándor wrote a letter to his colleague at the Kőbánya Savings Bank that he was at Horthy-liget camp. In the letter he asked that his writing and documents be saved. We don't know if he also wrote a letter to his family that did not arrive. A junior officer hid the documents in the rock cellar of the bank. They were never found, and the junior officer disappeared after being deported to a Russian prisoner of war camp.

In 1945, János Fóthy, a journalist of *Pesti Hírlap* and fellow prisoner with Sándor, published a book about his experiences at Horthy-liget. (see **Horthy-liget, the Hungarian Devil's Island on page 218**). András summarized the relevant narrative. Fóthy wrote that Sándor was a clerk for their unit, responsible for administrative tasks. He also wrote that Sándor was extremely popular. On July 15th trucks arrived at the camp. It was the last time Fóthy saw Sándor. My grandfather Sándor was one of 35 lawyers sent to Auschwitz. This was confirmed by the German records.

Sándor's 55th birthday fell on August 23, 1944. Not having heard from or about him for almost two months, Bözsi was overcome with fear and

My grandfather Sándor at his favorite restaurant, Gundel, circa 1935.

dread. Gábor wrote that Bözsi fasted all day. She continued to fast on his birthday for years.

Bözsi's losses were wrenching. In April, her husband was jailed and tortured. In May, her only son (my father) left for forced labor camp. In June, she was driven out of her home to live in a yellow star house. She, her mother (Margit), and other members of her extended family were under constant threat of deportation. But she had friends and relatives who checked in on her, including Zoltán, Sándor's brother, who was being hidden by his Christian wife.

Bözsi did not know that in July 1944 Sándor was deported to Auschwitz. After a hellish three-day journey, he arrived in Auschwitz on July 22nd. Although he was 55 years old, he survived the selection for life or death directed by Dr. Josef Mengele. Most men over 50 were sent to the gas chamber immediately upon arrival at the concentration camp. On September 29th he was transported from Auschwitz 520 miles west to Dachau (Germany). I found his identification numbers in the Arolsen Archives: prisoner number 112184; ID number 60683. Had he been tattooed with this number? Why was he transferred? We will never know.

I remembered my mother telling me an acquaintance remembered Sándor from Dachau and reported that he was truly kind. Sándor had been assigned a job to peel potatoes. He was able to sneak food and clothing for his fellow inmates. The acquaintance also told my grandmother that he died of a heart attack at Dachau on liberation day. But the story was more complicated than that.

According to the Arolsen Archives and the Dachau Concentration Camp Records, my grandfather was on a transport list to Ötztal. By the end of April 1945, US troops were closing in on Dachau. Gestapo Chief Heinrich Himmler was determined that no prisoners fall into the hands of the enemy alive. On April 26th, the commandant of the camp forced 7,000 surviving inmates on a death march south to Ötztal, Austria.

By air, the distance between Dachau and Ötztal is 125 miles. But the journey, across the Alps, was cold, steep, and treacherous even for healthy and able-bodied men. It was remarkable that any prisoners, weakened by months or years of brutal treatment and starvation, survived this march. Thousands did not and were shot along the way.

Did Sándor die on the journey? Did he even go on the journey? His name was found on an alphabetical list by name, not prisoner number, thought to be created by the remaining prisoners for the American soldiers after they liberated Dachau on April 29th. His name also appeared on a list of patients sick with tuberculosis. Dachau prisoners were used as guinea pigs in many types of medical experiments. One was for tuberculosis; prisoners were deliberately infected with tuberculosis to test the efficacy of various pharmaceuticals.

Sándor's personal card issued in Dachau was found in the Arolsen Archives. It contains contradictory evidence; Ötztal is written on it, suggesting he was on the death march. Yet a red stamp indicates that he was delivered into the hands of the US Army.

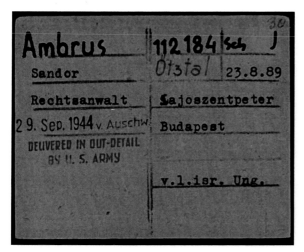

Sándor's personal card issued at the camp office in Dachau. Courtesy ITS Arolsen Archives.

There is no record of Sándor's death. His body was never found. I don't know how and when he died. But I do hope that he was in American hands. I hope he knew he was free and that he experienced acts of kindness in his final days. I hope someone called him by his name and restored dignity to his soul.

On November 2, 1945, the Bar Association removed the names of all its members who had not shown up for an identity check. Dr. Sándor Ambrus' name was removed in February 1946. On September 24, 1947, Dr. Antal Gratz, his colleague who was appointed custodian of his office, filled out an application to issue a death certificate. Under place of death was written "deportation." Under date of death was written April 30, 1945.

In 1950, the Hungarian Bar Association inaugurated two large plaques to commemorate the 800 former members who died in the war.

In September 2019, my sister and I visited the Hungarian Bar Association. We held back our tears as András pointed to Sándor's name on the left panel and to István Misner's name on the right panel.

My father rarely spoke about my grandfather's life, and he never spoke about his death. When I questioned my grandmother Bözsi, she told me that he was taken as a political prisoner and died in jail. She wore black for years. When I asked my mother about it, she told me that Bözsi was in mourning. Now I know why.

Remembrance Hall at the Budapest Bar Association. Photo: Levente Tóth, 2022.

ADLER LÁSZLÓ	BIN...
ADONYI JÁNOS PÁL	BIR...
ALGAI JÓZSEF	BEC...
ALTMANN ANDOR	BLA...
ALTMANN FERENC	BOD...
ALTMANN PÁL	BOG...
AMBRUS SÁNDOR	BOG...
ANDOR LÁSZLÓ	BOJ...
ANTAL PÁL	BOK...
APOR JÁNOS	BOL...
ARATÓ BÉLA	BOL...
ARJE SÁNDOR	BOL...
ATLASZ ISTVÁN ERVIN	BOS...
ÁRTÁNDI JÓZSEF	BŐH...
BACHRACH ALFRÉD	BRU...
BAK HENRIK	BRA...
BALASSA GYÖRGY	BRA...

MEZEI ENDRE	R...
MÉSZÖLY JENŐ	RÉ...
MIKLÓS GYÖRGY	RÉ...
MIKLÓS GYULA	RIC...
MIKLÓS ISTVÁN	RIE...
MIKLÓS LÁSZLÓ	ROI...
MISNER ISTVÁN	ROS...
IFJ. MOLNÁR DEZSŐ	ROS...
MOLNÁR MÁRTON	ROS...
MOLNÁR PÁL	ROT...
MUNCSIK SÁNDOR	RÓN...
MÜHLRÁD ARTUR	RÓN...
NAGY ARTUR	RÓZ...
NAGY ENDRE	RÓZ...
NAGY SALAMON SÁNDOR	RUI...
NATZLER ERVIN	SAC...
NEMES FRIGYES	SA...

Plaques honoring members lost during WWII. Sándor Ambrus is listed on the left, István Misner is listed on the right. Photo: Levente Tóth, 2022.

Rosenfeld Family: Talented Writers

Sándor's mother's maiden name was Rosenfeld. The Rosenfeld family had several published authors, including two women – a remarkable achievement for their time. It was exceedingly difficult for a woman to get published. Elvira Mihelfy, Sándor's stepsister, published three poetry books. Her book *Anica* is a compendium of poems about losing her daughter, aged 10.

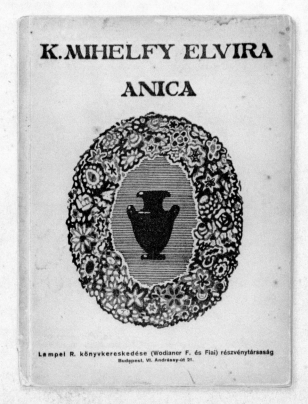

Cover of Elvira Mihelfy's book, *Anica*, published in 1914.

Bella Rosenfeld (1869 – 1908), Sándor's cousin, published a book titled *Women*. Bella was the first wife of Sándor Bródy (1863-1924), a novelist and playwright. When András discovered this connection, he exclaimed, "He is one of my favorite authors!" Apparently, Bella was even more talented than her husband. He wrote to her, "What I would not give if you could not write now, if I knew that you cannot write: I am jealous and scared of what enchanted me before – the writer in you. Someone who can correctly express feelings she does not feel: aren't you confused about yourself at times?" After a stormy relationship, they split. Bella died of pneumonia in 1908, two years after her book was published.

 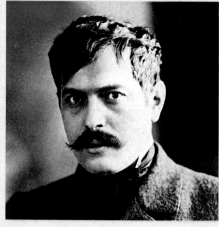

Bella Rosenfeld and her husband Sándor Bródy, circa 1890.

Horthy-liget, the Hungarian Devil's Island

János Fóthy, an outstanding journalist of Pesti Hírlap (The Pest Gazette), published a book in 1945, *Horthy-liget, the Hungarian Devil's Island*. He described how in early April 1944 intense bombing by the Allies destroyed the Dunai Airplane Factory. It was no longer capable of producing the German Messerschmitt aircraft.

The Minister of the Interior decided to make the Jewish elite "pay" for this destruction. They chose 83 lawyers, members of the press, and representatives from industry and finance. János Fóthy was one of the 83. My grandfather was another.

Fóthy's book, along with three accounts from witnesses (found on the DEGOB website), told the story. The Rökk Szilárd prison, Horthy-liget, and several other camps were under the command of Dr. Pál Ubrizsy, a 35-year-old policeman. He had unlimited power and influence despite his youth and low rank. A worker for the Jewish Council described him thus: "A sadistic hangman, who delighted in his power and in the torment of his victims. It is not needed to speak about Rökk Szilárd Street as the history of the damned institute has been described in numerous books and articles by the writers and journalists who stayed there."

As horrific as the conditions were at Rökk Szilárd Street, they were nothing compared to Horthy-liget. One witness called Horthy-liget the "worst chapter in the story of the interned in Hungary... they were kept in stalls, which were half ruined by the air raids." There was one faucet for several hundred people. Conditions were unthinkable. The prisoners wore the yellow star on the left and a tin flat plate covering half of their chest on which there was a diagonal yellow stripe and their prisoner number underneath. They worked 12 hours a day, clearing the debris from the site of the aircraft factory. After their workday, "Jews had to participate in a running contest including jumping over hurdles, to entertain the soldiers." Anyone who was unable to participate was brutally beaten.

I wanted to know the truth of my grandfather's death. Yet as I learned more, I struggled not to picture him in this nightmare. I hoped that Sándor, athletic and fit before the war, somehow avoided such beatings. I knew this was wishful thinking. Fóthy wrote, "The cruelest of all were the so-called factory inspectors who worked for counter-intelligence and who, equipped with guns and sticks, made people's lives a living hell... Anyone who attempted to escape was hanged."

FAMILY TREE

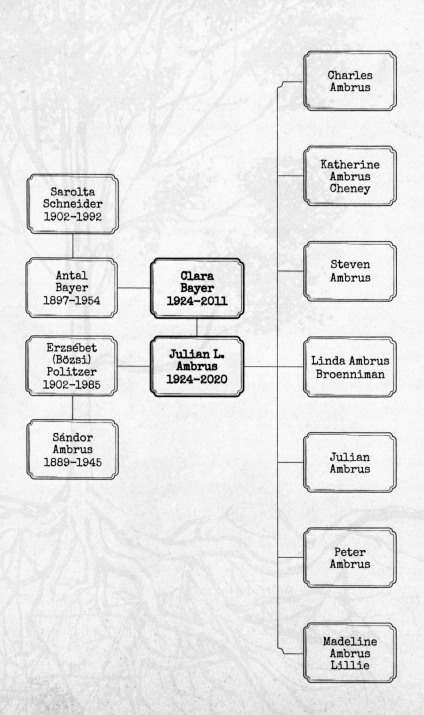

Sarolta Schneider 1902–1992

Antal Bayer 1897–1954

Erzsébet (Bözsi) Politzer 1902–1985

Sándor Ambrus 1889–1945

Clara Bayer 1924–2011

Julian L. Ambrus 1924–2020

Charles Ambrus

Katherine Ambrus Cheney

Steven Ambrus

Linda Ambrus Broenniman

Julian Ambrus

Peter Ambrus

Madeline Ambrus Lillie

Chapter 15

My Parents: Julian Ambrus and Clara Bayer

In writing this book, I moved back in time, beginning with family in the 1700s, eight generations before me, to those closer to the present. Their poignant stories, especially those of my parents and grandmother, the people I thought I knew best, were revelations. They had lived lives I could not have imagined. Loving them did not mean really knowing them. I was especially shocked by how little I knew about my parents, Clara Bayer Ambrus (1924-2011) and Julian Ambrus (1924-2020).

1942: Young Love

My parents started medical school in Budapest in the fall of 1942, before the war had reached the city. The school system there differed from the US in that students went directly into medical or law school, or other fields, without first attending an undergraduate program.

My mother told me the story of their first encounter when we visited Hungary in 1990.

Several months after school began, my mother was in the chemistry lab. The students had to make notes of the steps used in the assigned experiments. When her pencil broke, she asked a friend to borrow one. He mentioned that another student would be delighted to give her one, and added that this other student frequently asked about her, hoping to be introduced. That student was my father.

After the chemistry lab, my father asked my mother permission to accompany her home. "During our walk, he described the kind of person he was going to marry. It was my description. I found it surprising and unsettling. I thought to myself, who did he think he was. I don't even know him."

A year and a half later, in February 1944, in the middle of their second year, my father proposed to my mother. In the biology building, they kissed for the first time. They were 19 years old.

One month later, on March 18, 1944, the Germans occupied Hungary. Life became chaotic. Frequent sirens announced the allied bombings. One day, as the engaged couple was walking, the sirens went off and they ran to the nearest bomb shelter. When the air raid ended, my father introduced my mother to the other shelter seekers. They were his family members. The bomb shelter, in the basement of what mother thought was a large apartment building, was in the basement of his home on Teréz körút, and each apartment was occupied by a member of his family.

My grandfather Sándor invited my mother upstairs. He did not know that my father had proposed to her. It was the first and only occasion my mother got to spend time with her future father-in-law. At first, she was intimidated. He was strong, self-confident, and imposing. But he put her at ease with his sense of humor and genuine interest in her dreams. She enjoyed meeting this handsome, charming, and distinguished man. She had never met anyone like him.

My mother had known nothing about my father's upbringing. Because he dressed shabbily and always seemed a little unkempt, she thought he came from a poor family. I don't know if, at the time, she knew he was Jewish. He was attending medical school, when, according to the anti-Jewish laws, the quota for Jews accepted to university was miniscule. My mother was Catholic. Relationships between Christians and Jews had been ruled illegal in August 1941, when the third anti-Jewish law banned marriage and extramarital sex between Jews and non-Jews.

If she hadn't known before about her fiancée being Jewish, by April 5, 1944, a few weeks after the air raid incident, she would because my father, together with all Jews, had to wear the yellow star. On April 7th, he had to turn in his bicycle, a high school graduation present from Aunt Lili and Uncle Alfréd (Gábor's parents). Along with bicycles, Jews had to surrender their cars, gold, silver, jewelry, radios, and phones. Each day brought new and more onerous decrees restricting Jews' livelihood and daily existence. Food rations were reduced, and Jews could only shop at specified times, limited to two hours per day. My father was forbidden from going to the cinema, theater, restaurants, and from taking walks in Budapest's many parks. I try to imagine them robbed of their youthful fun, their favorite activities eliminated: hiking, visiting cafés in Buda, and going to the cinema.

My father's world was crumbling around him. A few weeks later, on April 27th he said goodbye to his father who was taken to the Gestapo prison. Two weeks later he received a draft notice for forced labor, requiring him to report on May 15th. Two days before he was scheduled to leave, on May 13th, he and my mother told their families that they were engaged. Even worry and dread could not undo love.

My mother, Clara, and my father, Julian, before they were married, circa 1943.

A Pact of Silence

My father kept his silence about forced labor camp. We first learned that he had been conscripted when András translated some documents that were in the box. Letters my parents wrote to each other during that time revealed a little more. We also learned bits and pieces from Gábor's book and from correspondence between my father and the son of a fellow laborer.

On the appointed day, my father was taken to a camp in Süvete (Šivetice, Slovakia). They worked at the Ládi timber yard in the Bükk mountains, a 90-minute train ride from Süvete. A southward projecting spur of the

Carpathian Mountains in northeastern Hungary, the area is one of the most rugged in all of Hungary. They carried large logs and wooden boards to the trains. It was hard physical labor.

They faced 17-hour work days, awakening at 4:30 AM and returning to the barracks after 9:30 PM. "We are living here like animals," my father wrote in a letter to my mother on June 11th. My father closed every letter with: "Kissing you a million times."

Gábor wrote in his book that my father returned to Budapest around November 1st. This was inconsistent with documents in the box (rescued from my parents' home) that listed my father's last day of labor service as January 15, 1945 – two and a half months later. Whatever happened between those dates changed the course of my father's life, and I wanted to know what it was. With András' help, we puzzled out events as best we could.

In October, six men escaped from the labor camp. One of them was my father. What events led to their escape? How did they make their way through the formidable terrain and treacherous populace to safety? My father took those details to the grave. It seemed the six men had made a pact of silence.

I found some correspondence between my father and Jean-Paul Herman. Jean-Paul was the son of József (Maxi) Herman, also one of the six. My father had written that when they escaped, they hid in the forest for several days. Twice they were caught by patrols and taken to nearby towns.

From their correspondence, I learned the names of the other men. One was Mihály Bächer (1924-1993), who later became a famous pianist known for his Liszt and Beethoven interpretations. András found out that his son Iván, who died in 2013, had written a short story about his father, disguising names, dates, and places. One passage described that there were few survivors from the labor camp where his father served. No other specifics.

The Ládi timber yard in the Bükk mountains.

Another of the six included András Bródy (1924-2010), who became a world-famous economist/mathematician. András Gyekiczki (my research partner) knew his son, János Bródy, one of Hungary's most beloved and celebrated composers/lyricists and founder of the band "Illés" in the 1960s. When András questioned him, János knew nothing beyond what was published on his father's website.

> He owed his life to blind luck, because once he walked out into the woods, the camp was hit by a bomb. Everyone in the camp was lost. He survived. He escaped soon after.

Somehow, they obtained falsified army documents giving them permission to travel. How they got these documents and money for the train to Budapest is a mystery.

But they were headed home. On the train, a German officer sat down opposite Maxi. They began to talk in German about all kinds of things. This saved Maxi and the others. When the police came into the compartment, they didn't bother to ask for papers because of the friendly chatter with the German officer. The officer was so charmed by Maxi that, upon arriving in Budapest, he said he wished that all Hungarians were like him.

When they arrived in Budapest the others had hiding places. Because Maxi had no place to go, my father invited him to stay with my mother.

Clara Hides Jews in the Factory

Shortly before my father reported to labor camp, in the spring of 1944, my mother and her family (her mother and father, Sári and Antal Bayer, and her younger brother, Ivan) moved into an abandoned factory complex. Circumstances surrounding this move happened because of the friendship between my mother and Éva Fisher, who was Jewish.

The two young women had been inseparable friends since grammar school. Éva was in love with Rabbi Béla Eisenberg. She and Béla needed a hiding place. And so did the rabbi's friend, Ármin Grószmann, a Polish Jew, who owned a factory which had been shut down. The factory seemed the perfect place to hide, but they needed someone like my mother, a Christian and therefore above suspicion, to be living there.

When Éva asked, my mother did not hesitate to hide them. I don't know how her mother, my grandmother Sári, felt, undoubtedly understanding the risks. She may have needed a place to live. Her husband had been arrested on suspicion of passing intelligence via a short-wave radio operated from their apartment. He was imprisoned and tortured. Freed after a month, he moved into the factory complex with them.

The large property included a main house, a separate servant's quarters, and a factory building. My mother could hide not only Ármin, Rabbi Eisenberg and Éva, but also their families. She also hid my grandmother Bözsi and someone named Uncle Tomi. My father and Maxi, after they escaped from the labor camp in late October 1944, returned to Budapest and hid there as well. When I met with Éva in 2007, she told me that several others came and went from hiding at the factory grounds.

A tall fence surrounded the property and kept it safe from prying eyes. Two large dogs guarded it and barked ferociously if strangers approached. Almost daily, Arrow Cross soldiers knocked on the large iron gate to the entrance, determined to search the house. My mother or her mother, Sári, would come to the gate, as slowly as possible, and ask the soldiers if they could lock up the dogs before opening the door. This allowed time for everyone to get to their hiding places.

The Americans usually bombed in the morning and the British in the evening, almost on schedule. That changed in the late fall of 1944; then the Russians took over the bombing. The Russians did not stick to a schedule, bombing indiscriminately day and night. The dogs became confused.

One day, after intense bombing, the knock at the gate came without warning. The dogs hadn't barked. Everyone scrambled, barely reaching their hiding places when the Arrow Cross soldiers marched in. My mother and Sári feigned calm, as they led them into the kitchen. Suddenly, my mother spotted the rabbi's siddur (a Jewish prayer book) on a countertop in full view. She moved toward it, signaling to Sári to distract the soldiers. When their attentions turned to Sári, my mother grabbed the siddur and pulled it into her lap. Once the soldiers searched the next room, she hid it in a safe place. She knew that if they had seen that book, they would have torn the buildings apart and all would have been shot.

As winter approached, supplies grew scarce. Food was rationed according to the number of family members. My mother, her parents and brother were registered as a family of four. They took turns waiting in long lines at the store, but often returned home with almost nothing to feed themselves or the others who hid there. Hunger was a constant companion, as was the bombing, which forced people standing in lines to seek shelter. Alternatively, one could buy bread on the black market and risk getting shot. The weather turned bitter cold, and dead bodies littered the streets.

The day after Christmas, the Russian army circled Budapest in a siege that would last seven weeks. They cut off electricity, which meant no light, no water, and no heat during one of the coldest winters in Hungary. Telephone service, too, was sporadic to non-existent. In the first two weeks of January, hand-to-hand combat in the streets made it too risky for anyone to venture out. Many Jews put the yellow stars back on their coats so Russian soldiers would not regard them as German enemies. They weren't sure who to be more scared of – the Arrow Cross with their rabid thirst for brutalizing the Jews or the Soviet soldiers who had a well-earned reputation for plundering, looting, and raping women.

The streets of Budapest during the siege, January 1945.
Fortepan / Vörös Hadsereg.

A Second Escape and a Wedding

On January 9, 1945, my father, Rabbi Eisenberg, and Maxi left the safety of the factory to search for food. Two Russian soldiers approached them and asked if they would help unload guns and ammunition in exchange for food. When they arrived at the railroad station it became evident that the Russians had misled them. Several captured SS soldiers were arriving in cattle wagons to be shipped to prisoner of war camps. The prisoner count did not match the paperwork. To avoid severe reprimand by their commanders, the Russian soldiers had searched for replacements – and found my father and his two friends. They were pushed into the cattle wagons together with the SS officers. Eventually, the three friends were marched to a Russian prisoner of war camp in Gödöllő, about 60 miles from Budapest.

We don't know how long they were held captive. According to my father, a woman doctor at the camp told them that the following day their destination was a Siberian labor camp. Upon hearing this, Rabbi Eisenberg started to yell. He yelled in Hungarian, he yelled in Yiddish, he yelled in every language he knew to get someone to understand his side of the story.

It turned out that one of their Russian captors was Jewish and understood Yiddish. As a fellow Jew, the Russian soldier decided to help. He gave them official documents stamped with notification that they were sanctioned by the Russian government. He suggested that they go to Szeged where there was less activity and Russian troops less prevalent. With the stamped documents, my father and his friends could move more freely, without the risk (or with reduced risk) of being seized.

The three men went to Szeged, on foot and by jumping on the backs of trains. Once they got there, Rabbi Eisenberg was determined to retrieve his family, despite the dangers of returning to Budapest. He arrived at the factory during the last week in January (1945) with the message that my father and Maxi were safe in Szeged and urged my mother to join him there. As it turned out, the medical school in Szeged had reopened and my father, focused on getting his medical degree at all costs, had enrolled. It was a wise decision. He didn't know it then, but three more months would pass before the medical school in Budapest re-opened.

Once it was rumored that the trains between Budapest and Szeged were running, my mother and Éva packed their backpacks with some clothing and what little food their parents forced on them. On February 2nd they left. Arriving at the train station, they were coerced by Russian soldiers into loading ammunitions. The last in line, my mother took all her money and gave it to the Russian commander, begging him to let them go. Left with no money, they walked to Szeged, trying to stay off the main highway and out of harm's way. It took them three days.

They arrived at the university and, by luck, spotted my father at the entrance. He ran to them and took my mother into his arms. Before the week was out, my father suggested to my mother that they marry as soon as possible, rather than wait. They had read an announcement that unmarried female medical students had to enlist in the Russian army to serve in Vienna where the fighting was still fierce. They went to the dean of the medical school and asked him to enroll my mother and Éva and to act as their guardian to approve their marriage, as they were still underage.

Five days after the unconditional surrender of Hungary, on February 18, 1945, my parents were married at the Votive Church in Szeged, one of the biggest cathedrals in Hungary. Éva, Maxi, and András Bródy were in attendance.

My father had converted in 1939, along with other family members because of antisemitism and the coming war. But I wondered when he decided to renounce his Judaism and hide his roots forever. Could it have been on his wedding day, in this grand cathedral?

From their first kiss in February 1944, as young medical students, until February 1945, the year had been one of intense transformation, for the country, for the family, and for them. They survived. Their love thrived. They would treat their survival as a precious gift. They would build new lives.

The Votive Church in Szeged where my parents were married in February 1945.
Wikipedia / Thaler Tamas.

A Return to Budapest

Two months later, at the end of April, my parents returned to Budapest to resume their medical studies there. They moved into Teréz körút, although the house was in shambles. Suitable living quarters were greatly reduced. I presumed that they moved in with my father's mother and grandmother – Bözsi and Margit.

It took months to unravel people's whereabouts. My father, only 20 years old, went to identify the body of his uncle István Misner from the mass grave in Csomád (described in **Chapter 13**). The body of his great-grandfather Ignácz Misner was in the mass grave in the Jewish Cemetery in Kerepesi street, Budapest, beyond identification and removal to the family tomb (described in Chapter 11). Not knowing how his father had died, (described in **Chapter 14**), must have been devastating. His mother, Bözsi, was deeply depressed. The sadness and anxiety must have been unbearable.

Members of my father's huge family, close and distant, had been lost. Friends had been lost. Nevertheless, my father, with my mother at his side, tried to focus on their future and their medical careers. They were committed to the betterment of mankind. Medical research was how they chose to serve.

The death rate in Budapest continued to spiral even though the war had ended. Worst of all, food was scarce. The university distributed baked beans or warm bean soup, one of the few staples available. (For the rest of their lives, my parents could not and would not eat beans.) My parents worked part time after school: my mother tutored students who were entering gymnasium (the European equivalent of high school) and my father was the doctor for the city's skating rink. Instead of money, they were paid in food, usually in bags of flour. Food was more valuable, as money was constantly devalued due to runaway inflation.

Hunger and cold were constant companions in the winter months. More than a year and a half after the end of the war, my mother still worried about the scarcity of food and heat.

My parents, Julian and Clara, 1945.

Medical School in Zurich

Two years later, in 1947, my father received a scholarship to study at the medical school at the University of Zurich. It would enable them to focus on their medical studies. My father left in the latter part of October. It took another six weeks until my mother could get the permits to leave.

During this brief separation, their correspondence was filled with discussions of their joint medical experiments and papers they were hoping to submit to medical journals. My mother teased that my father would be a recipient of the Nobel Prize in Physiology, like their professor, Albert Szent-Györgyi.

Their letters were also filled with my father's instructions to my mother for obtaining all the permits required – permits to purchase food, permits to get currency, proof of how money was obtained, permits to travel. The number of forms to be filled out and approvals to be acquired seemed endless.

I was not surprised to read about such bureaucracy when I learned about the communist takeover during those years. Once the Allied Control Commission (consisting of the US, Great Britain, France, and the Soviet Union) disbanded on September 15th, the communists aggressively consolidated their power by eliminating all opposition. In a precursor to the "show trials" of 1948-1950, on October 23rd, György Donáth, the leader of the Hungarian Community Organization, an anti-communist (and antisemitic), was hanged. My parents left Hungary just in time, before repressive measures prohibited anyone from leaving.

They graduated from the University of Zurich in May 1948 and completed a fellowship year at the Sorbonne (University of Paris) and the Pasteur Institute in Paris. They could not return to Hungary. I was unable to learn if the communists had put out a warrant for my father's arrest. Such measures were typical.

In 2019, I learned from my newly found cousin, Miklós Nicolson, (Zsigmond's great-grandson, see **Chapter 8**), that such was his father's fate. After the war, Miklós, then eight years old, had been part of a Red Cross program which took Hungarian children to Switzerland for three months recuperation. Miklós stayed on to attend a Swiss boarding school. When his father came to visit him, they learned that the communists had put a warrant out for his father's arrest. Miklós and his father emigrated to the US. Miklós' mother and younger brother were not allowed to leave Hungary and were expelled from their home in Budapest, as Margit and Bözsi had been. It wouldn't be until 1956 that they were able to join their family in the US, when Bözsi also came to join ours.

In October 1956, Hungarians revolted against the communist government, in what became known as the 1956 Revolution. There was a brief opening and over 200,000 Hungarians fled the country. In mid-November, the Soviets crushed the revolt and installed another repressive government, which ended all legal emigration until the 1990s, after the Iron Curtain fell.

Becoming Americans

In the rescued box (from the fire of my parents' home) I found a receipt for my parents' one-way tickets on the SS Italia from Naples to New York. They left on December 7, 1949, paying $526 for two tickets, a considerable amount of money for that time.

They had been recruited by Jefferson Medical College in Philadelphia to be assistant professors. While teaching they would also earn their PhDs in 1954. In Philadelphia, they started their family: my older sister, Madeline, and two older brothers, Peter and Julian, were born there.

In 1955, my parents were recruited by Roswell Park Memorial Cancer Institute, and they moved to Buffalo, New York. They would both go on to become highly respected doctors with significant research accomplishments. They would have four more children, including me, the fourth. Steven, Kathy, and Charlie were born after me, completing our family of seven children.

My parents' experience shaped their world view of education. They would become as highly educated as possible, and they would educate their children in the best way possible. They often told us that no matter what happens in the world, no one can take away what is in your mind.

It was no accident that medicine was their profession of choice. It is a completely mobile profession. It's not like law or running a factory or owning a shop. You couldn't lose what you knew. There is always a need for a doctor. They were determined to convince all their children to become doctors.

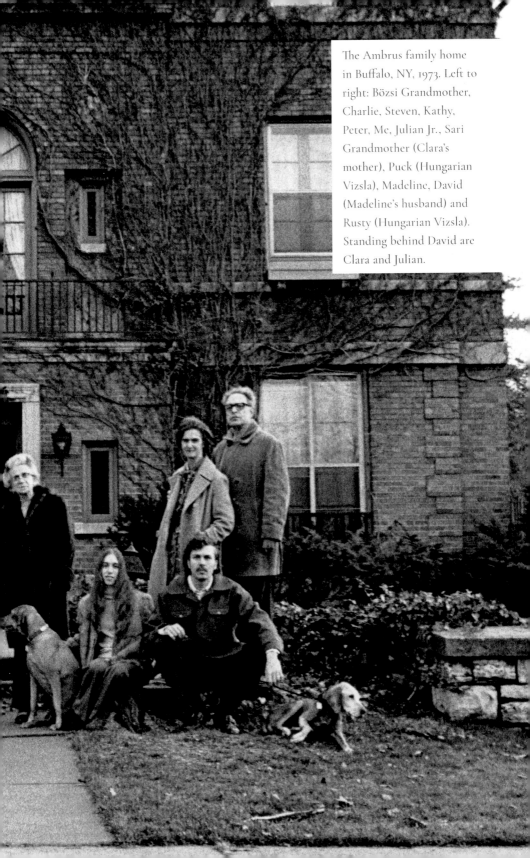

The Ambrus family home in Buffalo, NY, 1973. Left to right: Bözsi Grandmother, Charlie, Steven, Kathy, Peter, Me, Julian Jr., Sari Grandmother (Clara's mother), Puck (Hungarian Vizsla), Madeline, David (Madeline's husband) and Rusty (Hungarian Vizsla). Standing behind David are Clara and Julian.

My parents standing on
Fishers Bastion overlooking
the Parliament across the
Danube, circa 1991.

Julian Renounces Judaism: A Heritage Hidden

My father had a chance to start over in 1949, when they immigrated to the US. In his new country, no one knew him or his family name, or his religion. Yet in the US of the 1950s, antisemitism and anti-communism were still alive. Americans didn't trust Jews and they didn't trust foreigners. With his accent, he couldn't hide his foreign-ness. But he could hide his religious heritage. He did not want to face religious intolerance again. He chose to keep his Jewish roots secret from everyone including his children. He had created an identity he would not or could not let go of. He would protect it at all costs.

My mother and Grandmother Bözsi were keepers of my father's secrets, willing accomplices. We were raised Catholic, and the entire family, Grandmother Bözsi included, attended church every Sunday. I respect that they kept his secrets out of love for us and fear for our safety. But I wondered why they couldn't let go of those secrets, especially when we were grown, had discovered the truth, and the world had changed. My siblings and I could have learned so much more about our family, as seen through their eyes. I thought of what was lost because their voices were silenced.

Although my father refused to acknowledge his religion, he never forgot his love of Hungary. My parents' and grandmother's deep affection for their homeland was always expressed in grandiose terms. No matter how successful their American lives, I felt they viewed all things Hungarian as somehow superior. Not surprisingly, my parents supported and hired Hungarians whenever they could – as lab technicians, researchers, secretaries, custodians.

In the 1980s and 1990s, my parents returned to Hungary several times. A few visits were for medical meetings, but more often the visits were to show their children and grandchildren where they grew up. I remember my parents' excitement when their high schools held class reunions and they reconnected with classmates from around the world. Their proudest achievement, however, occurred when they were inducted into the Hungarian Academy of Sciences, one of the most prestigious societies in Hungary.

I travelled with them twice, in 1984 and 1990. On my second visit in 1990, having learned the truth about my heritage, I was able to ask my mother questions. She opened up, and shared with me quite a bit, or so

I thought. But not all of it was accurate or complete. Out of love for my father, she had safeguarded his deepest secrets.

Clara: Righteous Among the Nations

I came to learn that my mother also safeguarded her own secrets. I remember during our visit of 1990 that she told me, with considerable hesitation, that she "hid some people." Her humility gave no indication of the enormity of what she had done.

When I received the invitation from the Israeli consulate that she was to be honored as one of the "Righteous Among the Nations" (see **Chapter 1**), I was baffled. I had no idea what Righteous Among the Nations meant. At first, I thought it was something to do with the Christian right, an ideology my mother and I abhorred, though why it would come from the Israeli consulate I couldn't fathom.

My friend Yona corrected me. She told me, "'Righteous Among the Nations' is a great honor given to non-Jews who took great risks to save Jews during the Holocaust." I found the Yad Vashem website, the organization that provides the awards on behalf of the State of Israel. It states:

> In a world of total moral collapse there was a small minority who mustered extraordinary courage to uphold human values. These were the Righteous Among the Nations. They stand in stark contrast to the mainstream of indifference and hostility that prevailed during the Holocaust. Contrary to the general trend, these rescuers regarded the Jews as fellow human beings who came within the bounds of their universe of obligation.

At the ceremony, Ambassador Arye Mekel, the Israeli diplomat who is the son of Holocaust survivors, presented my mother with a medal and a certificate of honor after a moving speech. My mother, suffering from the advanced stages of Alzheimer's, was unable to read or comprehend what she heard. My father gave her acceptance speech. His speech was inspirational. But he omitted a vital fact – that he was Jewish and that she had hidden him.

כל המקיים נפש אחת כאילו קיים עולם מלא

WHOEVER SAVES ONE LIFE IS AS THOUGH HE HAD SAVED THE ENTIRE WORLD

כל המקיים נפש אחת כאילו קיים עולם מלא

WHOEVER SAVES ONE LIFE IS AS THOUGH HE HAD SAVED THE ENTIRE WORLD

בזכירה סוד הגאולה
(הבעש"ט)
Remembrance is the Secret of Redemption
(Baal-Shem-Tov)

תעודת כבוד

Certificate of Honour

THIS IS TO CERTIFY THAT IN ITS SESSION OF JANUARY 29, 2006 THE COMMISSION FOR THE DESIGNATION OF THE RIGHTEOUS, ESTABLISHED BY YAD VASHEM, THE HOLOCAUST HEROES' & MARTYRS' REMEMBRANCE AUTHORITY, ON THE BASIS OF EVIDENCE PRESENTED BEFORE IT, HAS DECIDED TO HONOUR

Clara Ambrus-Bayer

WHO, DURING THE HOLOCAUST PERIOD IN EUROPE, RISKED HER LIFE TO SAVE PERSECUTED JEWS.

THE COMMISSION, THEREFORE, HAS ACCORDED HER THE MEDAL OF THE RIGHTEOUS AMONG THE NATIONS.

HER NAME SHALL BE FOREVER ENGRAVED ON THE HONOUR WALL IN THE GARDEN OF THE RIGHTEOUS, AT YAD VASHEM, JERUSALEM.

וזאת לתעודה שבישיבתה מיום כט טבת תשס"ו החליטה הועדה לציון חסידי אומות העולם שליד רשות הזיכרון יד ושם על יסוד עדויות שהובאו לפניה, לתת כבוד ויקר ל

קלרה אמברוס-באייר

על אשר בשנות השואה באירופה שמה נפשה בכפה להצלת יהודים נרדפים מידי רודפיהם ולהעניק לה את המדליה לחסידי אומות העולם.

שמה יונצח לעד על לוח-כבוד בחורשת חסידי אומות העולם ביד ושם.

Jerusalem, Israel
APRIL 30, 2006

ניתן היום בירושלים
ב אייר תשס"ו

AVNER SHALEV אבנר שלו
בשם רשות הזיכרון יד-ושם
ON BEHALF OF THE YAD VASHEM DIRECTORATE

JACOB TÜRKEL יעקב טירקל
בשם הועדה לציון חסידי אומות העולם
ON BEHALF OF THE COMMISSION FOR THE DESIGNATION OF THE RIGHTEOUS

At the Yad Vashem ceremony in New York City, left to right: my father, my mother, Ambassador Arye Mekel, Consul General of Israel, and Ambassador Gábor Horváth, Consul General of Hungary.

After the speeches, the reporters hovered around my mother. I don't know if she understood anything about the honor she had received or why she was getting so much attention. She was able to smile, say thank you, and in response to one reporter's question replied, "I did what any decent human being would do."

I was astounded. She had been so absent, lost from her life and ours for so long. Yet for a fleeting moment she was there, the Clara Ambrus we knew; the woman whose courage made it possible for my father and my siblings to stand with her now, to have the lives we lived. That moment revealed the essence of her character – her bravery and fundamental decency, the humanity that still animated her, despite her diminished powers. Alzheimer's could not erase that. It is a memory of her I will always cherish.

My mother passed away in 2011 at age 86, the result of the fire in their home. My father lived nine more years after my mother died. He believed that his and my mother's survival during World War II was a miracle, and in many ways it was. Not only had they cheated death numerous times, but they also became accomplished doctors and scientists, contributing members of society. On January 14, 2020, my father, 95 years old, died peacefully in his home.

Certificate honoring my mother, Clara Ambrus, as Righteous Among the Nations.

Epilogue

In November 2021, a few months after the Politzer Saga Exhibit opened, I was on a zoom call with Zsuzsa Toronyi, Director of the Hungarian Museum and Archives, and some historians. Zsuzsa introduced me as a descendant of the Politzers. She was right. I am the great-great-great-great-granddaughter of Ábrahám Politzer. After all the searching and finding of family, I knew that. But when I heard the words said out loud, my connection to them felt real for the first time. I could feel those roots in my bones. These were the people who came before me and my parents. This was my family.

I am also the great-granddaughter of Margit Misner Politzer and the grand-niece of Lili Politzer Virány (Margit's daughter and my grandmother Bözsi's sister). The three middle names I had been given at birth – Clara (after my mother), Margaret (after Margit), and Livia (after Lili) – made sense now. I know who I was named after because I know who they were. Now that I have found them, I long to say their names out loud – a way to hold a place for them in my world.

Bringing their stories to light, allowed me to honor their memories and to experience the true meaning of the Jewish expression of condolence,

"May their memory be for a blessing."

For the dead and the living, we must bear witness.
Not only are we responsible for the memories of the dead,
we are responsible for what we do with those memories.

"

ELIE WIESEL

May Their Memory Be For A Blessing

Sándor Ambrus, my grandfather

Zoltán Ambrus, my grand-uncle, Sándor's brother

Irma Glück Engel, my grand-aunt, Sándor's sister

Gizella Misner Tibold, my great-aunt, sister to Margit Misner Politzer

Frédéric Tibold, my great-uncle, husband of Gizella Misner Tibold

István Misner, my great-uncle, brother of Margit Misner Politzer

Ignácz Misner, my great-great-grandfather and husband of Jozefa Politzer

Sarolta Misner, Ignácz Misner's niece

Bertha Goldschmeid Politzer, wife of Mihaly Politzer (brother of Jozefa Politzer Misner)

Ilona Politzer, daughter of Bertha and Mihaly Politzer

Raoul Barber, son of Ilona Politzer (Jozefa Politzer Misner's sister) and Izidor Barber

Maxine Müller, daughter of Gizella Barber (Ilona Politzer's daughter) and Leo Müller

Frédéric Hellsinger, son of Rosa Politzer (Maurus Politzer's daughter) and Sigmund Hellsinger

Bertha Politzer Herrmann, daughter of Illés Politzer

Clara Politzer, daughter of Albert Politzer (son of Bernát Politzer) and Fanny Friedmann

Endre Kovács, son of Hermine Politzer (daughter of Bernát Politzer) and Mathias Kovács

Aladár Politzer, son of Farkas Politzer and Karolin Esztreicher

Kornél Török, son of Zsigmond Politzer and Irma Pulitzer

Arthur Török, son of Zsigmond Politzer and Irma Pulitzer

Frédéric Török, son of Arthur Török and Frederica Koller

Victor Török, son of Zsigmond Politzer and Irma Pulitzer

Paul Török, son of Zsigmond Politzer and Irma Pulitzer

Béla Lederer, son of Margaret Politzer (Zsigmond Politzer's daughter) and Laszlo Lederer

Leo Politzer, son of Gusztav and Ernesztin Politzer

Frank Alberti, son of Gusztav and Ernesztin Politzer

George Benes, son of Gisella Politzer (daughter of Gusztav Politzer) and Anthony Benes

Family members named here were confirmed to have been killed in the Holocaust.

Works Consulted

Applebaum, Anne. *The Crushing of Eastern Europe, 1944-1956*, New York: Knopf Doubleday Publishing Group, 2013

Bodó, Béla. *The White Terror: Antisemitic and Political Violence in Hungary, 1919-1921 (Mass Violence in Modern History)*, New York: Routledge, 2019.

Büchler, Zsigmond. *Albertii-Irsai Izraelita Hitközség es Chevra Kadisa*, Nagyvárad, Hungary: Nyomatott Rubinstein Vilmos Kőnyvnyomdájában, 1909.

Day, Carolyn. *Consumptive Chic: A History of Fashion, Beauty and Disease*, New York: Bloomsbury Visual Arts, 2020.

DEGOB (National Committee for Attending Deportees). (n.d.). *Recollections of the Holocaust – The World's Most Extensive Testimonial Site.* http://www.degob.org/index.php?extsearch

Freifeld, Alice. *Nationalism and the Crowd in Liberal Hungary, 1848-1914.* Baltimore, MD: Johns Hopkins University Press, 2000.

Frojimovics, Kinga, Komoróczy, Géza, Pusztai, Viktória and Strbik, Andrea. *Jewish Budapest: Monuments, Rites, History.* Translated by Vera Szabó. Budapest, Hungary: Central European Press, 1999.

Gluck, Mary. *The Invisible Jewish Budapest: Metropolitan Culture at the Fin De Siècle.* Madison, WI: University of Wisconsin Press, 2016.

Miller Michael Laurence. *Rabbis and Revolution: The Jews of Moravia in the Age of Emancipation.* Stanford, CA: Stanford University Press, 2011.

Jewish Virtual Library, A Project of AICE. (n.d.). *Virtual Jewish World: Moravia, Czech Republic.* https://www.jewishvirtuallibrary.org/moravia

Kann, Robert A. *A History of the Habsburg Empire, 1526-1918*. Berkeley, CA: University of California Press, 1980.

Konrád, M. (2014). The Social Integration of the Jewish Upper Bourgeoisie in the Hungarian Traditional Elites: A Survey of the Period from the Reform Era to World War I. *Hungarian Historical Review.* 3(4):818-849

Lendvai, Paul. *The Hungarians: A Thousand Years of Victory in Defeat.* Translated by Ann Major. Princeton, NJ: Princeton University Press, 2003.

Lukacs, John. *Budapest 1900: A Historical Portrait of a City and Its Culture,* New York: Grove Press, 1988.

McCagg, William O. Jr. *A History of Habsburg Jews, 1670-1918*. Bloomington, IN: Indiana University Press, 1989.

McCagg, William O. Jr. *Jewish Nobles and Geniuses in Modern Hungary.* New York: Columbia University Press, 1972.

Medical University of Vienna. (n.d.). *Glorious Peaks and Painful Depths – Viennese Medicine.* https://www.meduniwien.ac.at/web/en/about-us/history/viennese-medicin-and-the-meduni-vienna/

Molnos, Peter. *Passion and Knowledge: The Bedő Collection and Its Place in the History of Hungarian Art Collecting,* Budapest, Hungary: Kieselbach Gallery and Auction House, 2010.

Morton, Frederic. *A Nervous Splendor: Vienna 1888/1889.* London: Penguin Books, 1980.

Nemes, Robert. *The Once and Future Budapest,* DeKalb, IL: Northern Illinois University Press, 2005.

Mudry, Albert. *Adam Politzer: A Life for Otology,* Amsterdam: Wayenborgh Publications, 2010.

OSA (Open Society Archives) Archivum, (n.d.). *Yellow Star Houses,* http://www.yellowstarhouses.org/#

Pappas, D. Sr., Pappas, D. Jr., McGuinn, M. (1999). Adam Politzer as an Art Collector. *Otolaryngology–Head and Neck Surgery.* 121(6):772-775.

Soros, Tivadar, Masquerade: *Dancing Around Death in Nazi-Occupied Hungary,* Translated by Humphrey Tonkin. New York: Arcade Publishing, 2001.

Spiel, Hilde. *Fanny von Arnstein: A Daughter of the Enlightenment, 1758–1818.* Translated by Christine Shuttleworth. New York: Berg, 1991; orig. 1978.

Stone, Robert. *Europe Transformed 1878-1919.* Oxford: Blackwell Publishers, 1984.

Stool, S., Kemper B. and Kemper M. (1975). Adam Politzer, Otology and the Centennial Exhibition of 1876. *The Laryngoscope,* 85(11): 1898-1904.

Szállási, A. (1979). Adalékok Politzer Professzor életéhez (Contributions to the Life of Professor Politzer). *Medical Weekly,* 120(36): 191-213.

Szép, Ernő, *The Smell of Humans: Memoir of the Holocaust in Hungary,* Translated by John Bátki. Budapest, Hungary: Central European University Press, 1994.

Ungváry, Krisztián, *The Siege of Budapest: One Hundred Days in WWII,* New Haven, CT: Yale University Press, 2006.

United States Holocaust Memorial Museum. (n.d.). *Holocaust Encyclopedia.* https://encyclopedia.ushmm.org/en

Vági, Zoltán, Csősz, László, Kádár, Gábor. *The Holocaust in Hungary: Evolution of a Genocide (Documenting Life and Destruction: Holocaust Sources in Context),* Lanham, MD: AltaMira Press, 2013.

YIVO Institute for Jewish Research. (n.d.). *The YIVO Encyclopedia of Jews in Eastern Europe.* https://yivoencyclopedia.org/

Zweig, Stefan. *The World of Yesterday.* Translated by Anthea Bell. incoln, NE: University of Nebraska Press, 2013.

Acknowledgments

The seeds for this book were planted by my dear friend, Yona Eichenbaum, in 1983. Shortly after we met in graduate school, Yona inquired about my family. I already knew about her family, that her parents were Jewish Holocaust survivors from Poland. When I told her that my paternal grandfather had been taken as a political prisoner and died in a concentration camp, she looked at me sadly and a little confused, but didn't ask more questions. Months later, when I learned that my father was Jewish, she suggested that I look more deeply into the story. Over the years, she continued, in only her subtle way, to encourage this endeavor, sending me books like The Lost: A Search for Six of Six Million by Daniel Mendelsohn.

When I began to search for the family I never knew, Yona not only became my most enthusiastic cheerleader, she became a collaborator. She listened to my ideas and read innumerable drafts, leading me to deeper clarity, offering suggestions and giving me honest feedback. She never shied away from asking every possible question of a sentence or a scene. She has a beautiful way of seeing things and expressing things, which made itself into the words, the pictures, and the design of this book. Any setbacks were met with encouragement and insistence that my disappeared family needed to be brought into the light. I am forever grateful for her friendship and her passion.

The box filled with family documents and photos that unlocked the past, was the critical catalyst for the search. I don't know how to express my gratitude to my sister, Madeline Lillie, for saving the box from our parents' home fire, for rediscovering it in the back of her closet, for sending it to me, and then for joining me on the voyage. I am grateful to her and her husband David, who generously contributed funds to support the research. I was thrilled when Madeline, and her three daughters, Christine, Sarah, and Karen agreed to be fellow explorers, traveling with me to Budapest in 2019. Their love and encouragement meant more than one can imagine. When you are searching for lost family, the family you know, the family you love, reminds you of how important it is to find them. Their faith in me to tell our family's story energized that long journey and helped me believe in myself.

The day spent with Anna Bayer to understand the contents of the box was a revelation. When Anna opened my eyes to Hungarian culture and the events of the Holocaust, I realized how little history I knew. She told me I needed an expert to interpret the documents within their historical context and introduced me to András Gyekiczki. Anna enthusiastically followed our progress and helped make new connections to break through a logjam. I am deeply indebted to her.

András' passion for the Politzer Story changed my world. It is why I dedicated this book to him. He had the generous assistance of many people: Peter Molnos, art historian, Katalin Erényi, the niece of Gábor Virány (my father's cousin), and Katalin Bardi, a translator and teacher. For those whose names were never shared with me, please know that I thank you.

A special thanks to Hédi Volosin, András' wife, for her valuable assistance in opening doors that enabled András to find answers he might not have found otherwise. She was a skillful editor, fine-tuning the use of words to ensure that they were aligned with Hungarian cultural norms. She continued to be a strong advocate for The Politzer Saga after András' death. Both Hédi and Katalin Bardi became close friends, and I will always treasure their friendship.

I am grateful to Zsuzsa Toronyi, Director of the Hungarian Jewish Museum and Archives. She was of immense help with András' research and so gracious in answering my many questions about Hungarian culture and history. She shared a vision that my family's stories could stimulate new awareness, especially among Hungarian Jews, about the power of ancestral legacies, and became the force behind the Politzer Saga Exhibit at the Rumbach Synagogue. She assembled a talented, committed team, headed by Peter Forgacs, to compose lyrical and artistically rendered films based on the stories in this book.

Herta Feely (Crysalis Editorial), my editor, embraced my story with enthusiasm and a deep understanding of why this journey was so important to me. She offered round after round of incisive feedback. And she encouraged me to make my voice heard, deftly helping me integrate my personal story with historical information. I am so grateful that Herta and her colleague, Emily Williamson, shared their invaluable insights with me.

The book design would never have crystalized without the dedication and brilliance of three enormously talented people: Tamás Sztaricskai, Levente Tóth, and Beatrix Kiss.

Tamás eagerly joined my Hungarian explorations, giving up weekends and holidays to search for my great-great-great-great-great-grandfather Móricz's grave and my great-great-grandfather Ignácz Misner's family farm. Tamás became an ardent supporter of the book, generously investing his time to make it a reality. He introduced me to Levente and Bea, oversaw our collaborations, and provided invaluable suggestions. I am deeply grateful for his dedication, generosity of spirit and endless energy.

One of the high points of my trip to Budapest was meeting Levente and Bea, a dynamic duo. They took time to understand my vision. And then went above and beyond, doing their own research and developing creative solutions that integrated text and photos into a cohesive whole I could not have envisioned without them. Our zoom calls were a delightful and fulfilling creative collaboration that I looked forward to every week — proof there can be joy in the journey.

I would like to thank Debbie Lange at BCG Publishers for believing in this book and taking risks for it that others would not. For this I am deeply indebted.

One of my unexpected joys from this journey was meeting new relatives: Miklos Nicolson and his wife Anne, György Máté and his significant other Ilona, his sister Zsuzsanna Méniet and her son Gyuszi, Thomas Virány, Gábor's cousin, and their nieces, Eszter Pataki and Klara Kovács. I am grateful for their hospitality and friendship. And for their generosity in sharing memories.

There are many friends and family members who provided their love, support, and encouragement. Emily Siegel magically provided just the right connections at the right time. Eileen Spinella patiently listened to me while walking our dogs. Eileen's brother Dan, a talented poet, read my first manuscript and gave me valuable suggestions. My brother, Charlie Ambrus, introduced me to his 2G group (second generation Holocaust survivors) where I shared some of the stories. Their interest provided encouragement at a time when I really needed it. My sister, Kathy Cheney, openly embraced my need to find the truth about our family and eagerly followed our progress every step of the way. Margaret and Laura Broenniman, my husband's daughters, and Meena and Maryam, our Afghan "adopted" daughters, held ringside seats to my trials and tribulations as they watched this book become a reality.

I don't know what I did in a previous life to deserve my husband, Ed Broenniman. There are no words to describe my gratitude for his love and unwavering support in this and in all my pursuits. He understood my need to find my family and write their stories. His infinite optimism kept me going, fueling the strength I needed to overcome obstacles. He has been there for me, through successes, disappointments, and failures. Everything is better when I am with him. He is a blessing and a source of inspiration and unending gratitude in my life.